HISTORIES FROM MY HEARTLAND

An Uncommon History of a Common American Family

 BY

SCOTT VAN ZANT

authorHOUSE®

AuthorHouse™
1663 Liberty Drive, Suite 200
Bloomington, IN 47403
www.authorhouse.com
Phone: 1-800-839-8640

First published by AuthorHouse 6/3/2008

ISBN: 978-1-4343-8264-1 (sc)

Library of Congress Control Number: 2008903771

Printed in the United States of America
Bloomington, Indiana

This book is printed on acid-free paper.

DEDICATION

For Brad and Kourt

And all the "players", past and present, that have contributed to our story.

CONTENTS

FOREWORD   IX

PART ONE: HISTORIES PAST   1

A Quilt to Warm the Heart   3

Fragments of a Legacy   15

A Soldier's Story   27

Silencing a Smile   37

The Last Museum Tour   53

A Baker's Life   59

Makin' the Salt Risin'   75

PART TWO: HISTORIES PRESENT   79

The Secret of Survival of Little Brothers   81

The Boys of Summer in Suburbia   89

The Scribbler Chronicles   99

The Dad Diaries   115

Sharing a Long Overdue Cup of Coffee   143

Drawing Pictures for My Kids   149

AFTERWORD   **157**

CAST OF PLAYERS   **159**

SOURCES   **173**

FOREWORD

Histories were those books that most of us avoided reading in school. They were the thick, heavy, classic texts that always looked impressive on the shelf, but felt strangely uncomfortable in your hands. For that reason, they usually stayed on the shelf, not only impressive but also imposing.

While we may have not been totally fair to histories in our youth (or even later), there may have been good unconscious reasoning behind our attitudes about leaving those books on the shelf. Maybe intuitively we realized that there was something fundamentally lacking in those typical histories. By their nature, they are accounts of those people, places, and events that were deemed "noteworthy" by some arbitrary and biased recorder. It is often said that "history is written by the victors", usually for the glorification of the winners and the denigration of the losers.

But most of history is made by players. The hunters, the farmers, the builders, the healers, the educators, the nurturers. It is through the dedicated and often forgotten service of these countless souls that the winners achieve the noteworthy status that their scribes so lovingly record. Life is indeed, as Shakespeare noted, "...a poor player who struts and frets his last hour upon the stage, and is heard no more." More histories should be about the players.

Traditional histories are often painted with a broad brush of garish color. Their accompanying sound track, if they had one, would be loud and raucous. Like the five-second sound bite on the evening news, they are meant to grab society's attention. They are a near infinite collection of bold type headlines. But most of the history of a man or woman is much more subtle, fragile and scarce. As Mark Twain noted in his autobiography,

> "...that is what a human life consists of – little incidents and big incidents, and they are the same size if we leave them alone. An autobiography that lets out the little things and enumerates only the big ones is no proper picture of a life

at all;   (a) life consists of ... feelings and ... interests, with here and there an incident apparently big or little to hang the feeling on."

More histories should be about feelings and interests, big and small, and their corresponding incidents that, along with the persons between the pages, the readers can hang their feelings on.

This is a collection of the feelings and interests, big and small, of several generations of players from not only America's heartland, but from my own as well.

PART ONE:
HISTORIES PAST

The Maxwell-Briscoe Forge, New Castle, Indiana,
circa 1910. Carl Van Zant is first on the left.

A QUILT TO WARM THE HEART

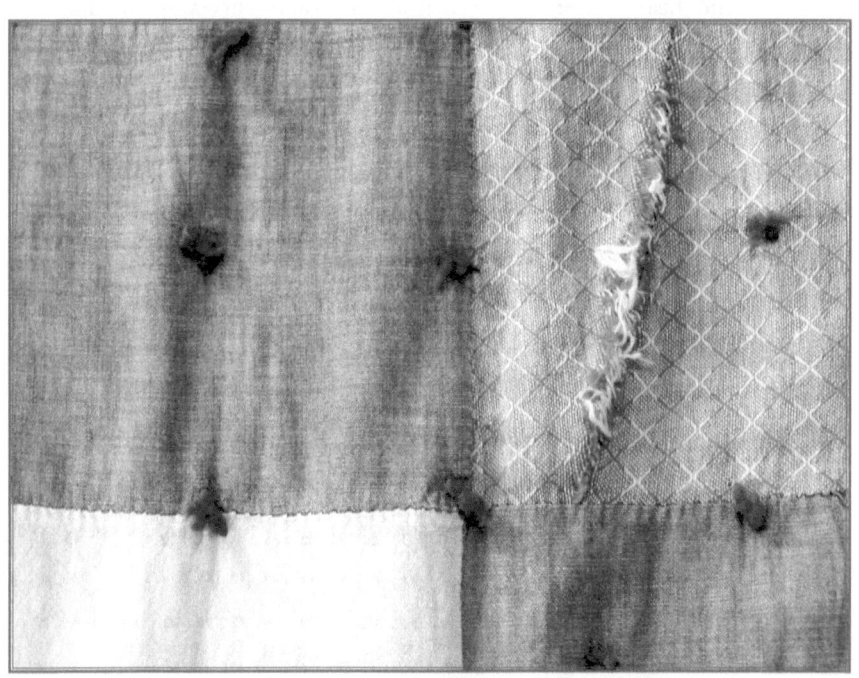

Detail of a quilt made by Marcella Van Zant.

The chill I felt as we walked up the cracked and crumbling concrete steps leading to the front door of my grandparent's home had nothing to do with the cold wind of that November afternoon. My Dad opened the wooden screen door, and placed the tarnished gold key in the equally tarnished lock of the large mahogany stained door. I looked over the doorway at the milky glass plaque with "GA Van Zant, 907 S. 19th" etched in blocked black letters that leaned to the left. As he turned the key and pushed the door open, I held the screen door as my Dad, Mom, and brother walked in.

I pushed the heavy door closed behind me, and surveyed the familiar surroundings. I knew every inch of that wide living room, and yet it didn't look right. It seemed small, dark, cold, and smelled like emptiness. "This isn't right," I thought to myself.

I looked to my left at the remnants of the huge fern in front of the south window. The fronds should be lush and arching toward the ceiling. The sun should be bathing it and the overstuffed brown velvet chair next to it. The house should be toasty (nearing tropically) warm, and on the opposite side of the room, the gently curved walnut clock in the center of the fireplace mantel should be sounding its distinctive rhythm. The accordion folded shade of the aged brass floor lamp that stood between the dark brick fireplace and her dark brown velvet chair should be gently glowing. She should be sitting in the chair, quietly looking up words for her crossword puzzle in her ancient red Webster's dictionary; the one whose spine and borders she had lovingly mended with bright red tape. There should be the faint hint of Sir Walter Raleigh pipe tobacco circling about the room as he rocked quietly in his green leather Lazy-Boy easy chair, leafing through his *True* magazine. In my mind's eye, focused from the past, that is how the room should and will forever look.

Dad walked between the massive dark wooden pillars that divided the living room from the dining room behind it, and turned up the thermostat until the furnace croaked to life. As we took off our coats and piled them on her empty chair, he said, "It should warm up pretty soon." He looked around somewhat bewildered, shook his head, and said with a sigh, "I don't know where to start."

Mom came over close to him, gently put her arm around his waist, and said, "Why don't you and the boys start here in the dining room, and I'll start in the kitchen."

It was a good plan, but he was right. Where do you start? Where do you start to sort out the tangible relics of over fifty years of living in a home? A home where he grew from a young boy to a young man. A home whose converted attic apartment served as their first home as a young married couple. A home where my brother lived the first years of his life, and where he and I spent countless hours relishing our youth.

Looking around the dining room, every nook and cranny could tell some cherished story from our past. While Grandpa was living, this room was Thanksgiving to me. The rectangular cherry table at the center of the room was covered with a white, embroidered table cloth, set for six with my Grandma's best china, crystal, and silver; the only day of the year the whole complement saw the light of day. Grandpa always sat at the south end of the table next to the doorway to their bedroom. He would be dressed in grey pants with red suspenders, a white shirt with gold cuff links, and a narrow dark tie with his Knights of Pythius tie clip. He and my Dad would always have a high ball in short glasses adorned with flying turkeys. I would rarely see my Grandfather drink any other time of the year. Grandma, usually wearing a flower printed dress with a matching cloth belt at the waist, sat at the north end of the table in front of the long buffet cabinet, not far from the door to the kitchen. The three windows behind her gave a fine view of the white siding of the neighbor's house, but sometimes hosted the show of seasonal snow showers. My Mom and I sat on the west side of the table, in front of the built in glass cabinets and dark wooden drawers that served as home for the china, crystal, silver, and table cloth the other 364 days of the year. Across from us over the bountiful table sat my Dad and brother. While I don't recall the typical menu, I seem to recall my brother and I usually each had a turkey leg, and Grandma always made green peas because it was my favorite vegetable. As my Grandpa never ate anything resembling a vegetable, I think she wanted to encourage this dietary behavior in her grandson.

In the southeast corner of the room was the old wooden phonograph, perched high on a cabinet with albums filled with old 78 rpm records stored below. I can still remember hearing the scratchy renditions of the big band sounds of Glen Miller and Tommy Dorsey, and laughing uncontrollably with my brother as we heard such Spike Jones classics as *Yingle Bells* and *We Spit Right in the Fuhrer's Face.*

Next to the phonograph sat a small grey toy chest that housed a treasure trove of trucks, tanks, planes, and army men. It was amazing the room was still standing considering all the battles it had hosted. Sitting on top of the toy chest was the "cut-out box". Whenever my brother and I visited, the dining room table often hosted a variety of races comprised of cars cut out of magazines. Formula One, Indy cars, and sports cars raced endless circles around the table. Fields of drivers of the past, present, and from our own fertile imaginations competed for mythical championships; the sole prize being the driver's name inscribed on a "List of Champions" paper carefully stored in the bottom of the box.

When the dining room table was not serving as a race course, battlefield, or the landing strip of an aircraft carrier in the stormy waters of the South Pacific, it served as a game room that rivaled the best that Vegas has to offer; for a kid that is. She loved to play cards, and she taught me solitaire, euchre, rum, poker, and some games I think she made up. She had little round cardboard discs of blue and red from some other game that were used as poker chips. I can recall many high stakes games; and oddly in this room the house usually lost. When we tired of cards, there were such diversions as Chinese checkers, Monopoly, and list games. My Grandma loved making lists; presidents, states of the union, state capitals, or whatever caught her fancy. I'm sure now she had some ulterior motive with her lists; history and geography lessons camouflaged as innocent recreations.

In the center of the buffet table sat the large, round glass candy dish. It was in the shape of a stunted cylinder with small rounded scallops all the way around. The matching lid had a thick bead of glass that served as a handle. The dish always had some treat for us; usually chocolate for my brother and candy orange slices for me (being the only kid on the planet who didn't like chocolate). There was also usually some Bazooka bubble gum, but we were rationed only one piece each visit.

If the vision of the room aroused all these memories for me, I could only imagine the torrent of thoughts going through Dad's head. I can remember Grandma telling me stories of him riding his tricycle around the dining room table; portending races to come in a new generation. I pictured him, a young boy with jet-black hair parted neatly on the left, sitting at the table, laboring over his homework. Grandma, thin and pretty, with curly black hair passes through to the kitchen, and as she departs, the young scholar pulls out a piece of white lined paper lying under his books that is filled with drawings of cars; another trait passed down to a later generation as well.

Dad sat down at the table and started leafing through a stack of papers he had retrieved from the long center drawer of the buffet table. He shook his head, and gave out a chuckle grounded more in perplexity than levity.

"I can't believe some of the things she kept," he said. "Look at this. Tax returns from the 50's. A log of volunteer hours at the Senior Center from ten years ago. A bill from when Dad was in the hospital in 1937…one hundred ninety two dollars for an eight day stay and a major operation…quite a bargain these days!"

Each drawer opened brought similar responses at the bizarre contents. Christmas cards decades old, and note pads and pencils with the compliments of businesses that no longer existed and political campaigns lost to history. There were several envelopes filled with newspaper clippings. One envelope marked "Rex" chronicled the achievements of my brother, while another labeled "Scott" contained clippings listing my locally acknowledged accomplishments. Other envelopes contained news items and pictures of a cavalcade of prominent personalities: John F. Kennedy, Danny Kaye, Jimmy Stewart, and John Lennon.

I found a pocket medical terminology dictionary from 1920, a vestige of my Grandma's career as a practical nurse. There was my Dad's first Catholic missal; a vestige of his early spiritual training that I came to find out later created in him more tension than comfort. And of course there were lists. A little palm-sized brown notebook contained the date, mailing address, and contents of each package sent to my Dad when he was in the service. Fruit, socks, cookies, and "the funnies" were frequent content items.

"Bob, come in here and take a look," Mom hollered from the kitchen. The three of us walked in as she pointed to a large open drawer of the built-in white metal kitchen cabinets. More head shaking from the three of us as we saw the thousands of pink packets of Sweet 'n Low and an equally bountiful number of plastic straws.

"And look at this," Mom added as she threw open the freezer compartment of the refrigerator to reveal, stacked like a child's blocks, dozens of eight ounce cartons of milk. "She must have brought this stuff home from the Senior Center. I'm sure this was stuff that was probably going to be thrown out, and she couldn't stand the thought of it going to waste."

I'm sure that was exactly it. Starting a life as a couple with a small son during the Depression, and later being a mother whose son and country struggled through World War II, she was like most of her era; appreciative of everything you had and ever resourceful. Other kitchen drawers revealed pieces of used aluminum foil, rolled up plastic bread bags, old cloth sugar and flour bags, and countless twist ties. Later in the fruit cellar we would find shelves full of preserved cherries that had to be decades old. The cherry tree in the back yard, which to me for years was merely a piece of gym apparatus to climb on and jump from, was a source of nature's bounty to my Grandma, even though I can never remember her serving cherries. But should the need arise, be it economic catastrophe or nuclear attack from the dreaded "Red Menace", my Grandma would have the cherries.

We all migrated through the small kitchen into the long and narrow breakfast room where my grandparents ate most of their meals. On the left wall at the end of the room, between Grandpa's chair and the small table that held the silver art deco style single slice toaster, was the door to the attic apartment. Still hanging on the door was last year's calendar from the Citizens State Bank of New Castle. The oversized calendar contained such essential daily information as the time of sunrise and sunset, as well as depicting the phases of the moon using smiling "man in the moon" icons. Immediately I was a little kid again, counting the days on the calendar until Christmas.

We made our way up the steep steps, and opened the wooden gate at the top of the landing. The apartment had long been vacant, but the closets served as a warehouse of old memories. Now vintage clothes of both my grandparents hung in the long walk-in closet in the bedroom. A door at the back of the closet opened into the unfinished part of the attic at the front of the house. Venturing in with a flashlight, we discovered a wooden child's rocking chair and a wooden toy trolley. In my mind, an even smaller version of my Dad sat on a flowered area carpet in the living room one floor below, playing master conductor of his busy red trolley.

At the end of the long, narrow closet sat a large black steamer trunk with brass accents and latches. Inside were several family photo albums filled with faces both strange and familiar. Dad picked up a heavy blue book entitled *A History of the United States*, and turned to the title page that contained the message "To Robert, Christmas 1938".

"I remember getting this from my Grandma and Grandpa Van Zant and being very disappointed," my Dad recalled. "I had hoped for some toy or something, and getting this book was quite a let down." I look closer, and on the inside cover someone had noted in pencil, "April 28, 1939: It snowed today." A meteorological anomaly anonymously noted.

The freezer of the apartment refrigerator yielded another store of long expired single serving milk cartons, and the closet on the landing housed a large, hand-made plywood storage chest that held a full-length fur coat. The coat must have been quite the fashion statement in the 1940's, and was actually rather out of character for my grandparents, as they were typically rather frugal. I can remember Dad saying how Grandpa always was worried about the price of things, rarely buying anything but the most economical of items, and going to several grocery stores to get the lowest prices for all the things on the grocery list. Growing up in this environment probably led to Dad's tendency of being more extravagant and enjoying his money. Although I never knew for sure, I can imagine Grandma and Grandpa probably thought Dad's purchases of boats, cars, and a vacation house trailer wasteful and excessive. My grandparents' single extravagance was an annual vacation to Florida in early December. I can still remember going with Dad to stoke their coal furnace while they were gone, and waiting eagerly for postcards of Florida beaches, and a brief chronicle of my Grandpa's fishing successes (or lack thereof).

Once again downstairs, I moved on to the bedroom at the rear of the house; my Dad's room. Just to the left at the end of the hallway that ran from the dining room, the room looked neatly ordered; just waiting for a guest to occupy it. A full sized bed with a walnut veneer headboard, and simple spindle footboard greeted you as you walked in, with a matching chest of drawers against the far wall, and a vanity off to the right. The only adornment on the wall to my left was a small, framed black and white picture of a cabin on a lake. Taken from a boat on the lake, a small boat motor filled the foreground, with the wake of the motorboat rippling into the center of the picture. A crudely typed title below the picture read "Churn'in George"; a reference to the lake that was the location of the weekly family vacations of my Dad's youth, and what he described as the best times of his life. On the back wall hung a framed black and white 8x10 of Dad in his army uniform, his beaming smile lighting up the picture.

I instinctively walked over and opened the top right hand drawer of the chest. I knew the contents almost by heart. Buttons from Dad's army uniform and from Grandpa's Fire Chief's uniform, the service star window pennant that hung in the front window while Dad was in the service, Dad's uniform decorations including his combat and good conduct badges. As a kid I came back here and investigated these items as if I were an archeologist on a dig, carefully replacing each into its original position after close and intent investigation. Even though I wasn't aware of it at the time, I think on some level I understood these tokens represented honor, dedication, and sacrifice. As such, they deserved, and were given, a special reverence.

I strolled back to the dining room, where my brother and my Dad sat at the table with various piles of papers, small boxes, and various odds and ends scattered about them. Mom was in the kitchen rummaging through drawers, sorting through long retired kitchen utensils and pots and pans. I went to the silverware drawer and located the 1933 Chicago World's Fair spoon, heralding a "Century of Progress". As I ran my fingers over the raised scroll work on the handle, I fondly recalled the many lunches I shared with Grandma and Grandpa in the breakfast room. On snow days from school, or if I was sick and couldn't go to school (but wasn't sick enough for Mom to stay home from work), I spent the day with Grandma and Grandpa. My traditional lunch was Chef-Boy-Arde Spaghetti with a side of bacon and a small cup of coffee. Though "doctored-up" with enough sugar and milk to make the drink hardly recognizable, it was the only time I was allowed to have coffee. A small burnt orange milk glass cup served as my mug (proportional to my small hand), and the World's Fair spoon clanked against the side as I over-stirred the concoction.

After helping Mom sort through the kitchenware, retaining a few wooden handled utensils I thought were both cool and useful as well as the spoon and cup, I returned to the dining room to find the piles on the table had both grown and multiplied. A large garbage bag sat half filled next to Dad. It was as if he was back at the Post Office, sorting mail again. Instead of sorting by names and addresses however, he was sorting by current relevance and past memories. While I know Dad was not the salvager that Grandma was, I was surprised at the number of items saved from seeing the inside of the garbage bag. With my collection from the kitchen, I began my own pile at one end of the buffet table. Before I knew it, my pile was growing as rapidly as those in front of Dad and my brother. The eclectic collection included my Grandpa's Fire Chief's hat, the buttons from the back room, my Grandma's medical dictionary, blue Ball canning jars (minus the cherries), and a bright gold Indiana State Fire Inspector's badge, with my Grandfather's name stamped on a banner at the top that was held in the talons of a golden eagle.

Without anyone noticing, Mom had finished her work in the kitchen and walked across the dining room into my Grandma's bedroom. I looked across the room and saw her piling hanging clothes onto the bed.

"Bob, did you know your Mother still has a lot of your Dad's clothes here?", she asked.

"No, I didn't," he responded absentmindedly, continuing his sorting.

I walked over to the bedroom to help Mom clear out the clothes in the closet. I carried several armloads of men's suits, pants, and shirts that had not been worn in the 13 years since my grandfather's death, and placed them in ordered piles on the bed. Sitting on the vanity next to the closet door, I noticed a small rectangular jewelry box I had gotten Grandma on my high school trip to Italy. The walnut box had a maple and walnut veneer design on the top, and was lined inside with red velvet. I recalled how she made such a scene when I gave it to her, just like she did with every gift, be it jewel or trinket, she ever got from my brother or me.

Just to the left of the vanity, sitting next to the doorway into the dining room, sat Grandma's cedar chest. About the width of a full sized bed, it had copper accents on the corners of the lid, and a large copper plate for the key lock on the front. I had never really noticed it before (probably because it usually had clothes piled on top of it), but the wood grain and frequent knotholes caught my eye. It reminded me of water ripples in a stream, moving past dark stones. I lifted the lid, and was embraced by the sweet woodsy aroma. Prominently displayed on the inside of the lid was a sign with large red lettering proclaiming "Genuine Tennessee Aromatic Red Cedar…A Positive Protection from Moth, Dust, and Damp." In one end of the chest sat a large bag full of scraps of material, and at the other end was a folded patchwork quilt.

I grabbed the quilt and plopped it on the piles of clothes on the bed. I carefully opened the quilt. The dark blue backing was faded and well worn. The front was a series of squares, each corner tied with thick green thread. It appeared the material came from a number of sources: denim pants, work shirts, dress shirts, old blankets. Several squares had small tears, revealing the batting below. The quilt was not familiar to either Mom or me, but it had obviously seen a lot of use at sometime in its life. Perhaps it had warmed my grandparents as they slept, or covered Dad during afternoon naps in his youth. Maybe it came from a friend or relative, and lived a life similar to Grandma's china, silver, and embroidered table clothes.

Whatever its true origins, it hit me that this quilt was the product of a lot of living and a lot of love. Each square told a unique story; a well lived life that ultimately gave way to time, only to be reborn as a new entity through the nurturing care of skilled and loving hands. In this quilt were uncounted workdays of many loved ones, days of warm comfort for children, and trips to holiday gatherings, weddings, funerals, and church picnics. In this quilt were miles of thread, pulled deftly by hand and secured carefully stitch-by-stitch. As I opened it to its full length and breadth, I got to thinking how this quilt was like a family, each square its own story, yet depending on the others to give it meaning and purpose. The whole ultimately is then lovingly held together by the miles of spiritual or cosmic thread.

It may seem silly, but at that moment the house seemed more like it should be. It seemed warm again, and not just because the furnace had been on for a couple of hours. The memories, and the realization and appreciation of the current day products that my grandparent's lives had led to, warmed me inside. Both he and she had returned, and I knew they would always be here, or wherever I would go. They would be here, because of all the times I had been here.

I reverently folded up the quilt and placed it in the cedar chest. I then gathered all the treasures from my memory pile and placed them in the chest as well. Mom had been going through the bag of scrap material, and decided she would take them home and start a quilt herself. Another square completed, and with it, the beginning of a new pattern.

FRAGMENTS OF A LEGACY

Fire Chief George A. Van Zant, New Castle, Indiana, circa 1945.

The pieces of cloth I had found in my Grandmother's cedar chest grabbed my imagination in a most unusual way. By themselves they were of little value; cut and torn pieces of well-worn material of various sizes, shapes and colors. Under any other circumstance I wouldn't have given them a second thought; something suitable only for the trash. But following her death, it took on a new and unexpected significance. It represented an unfinished project of a life just concluded. It made me think about how so many projects, ideas, and people are silently lost to time; blown into oblivion like the wind scattering the feathered seeds of a dandelion. It was that moment that I felt compelled to make sure that some of the ideas and people from my past and present needed to be remembered and held onto. And maybe, in the process, I might discover something more about myself.

Both my paternal and maternal legacies came from the obscurity of rural nineteenth century central Indiana. In 1837 the widow Nancy Runyon Van Zant moved to Henry County, Indiana from Hamilton County, Ohio with her four children. Her youngest son Nicholas was but four years old. Indiana was almost virgin frontier; collections of log cabins with the rare brick building at the center of the small towns that dotted the lush forests and fields. Many settlers to the "western lands" were people like Nancy; people in need of a new start. From lonely and difficult beginnings, she would be the first of seven generations of her family that would call Henry County, Indiana their home.

Other people seeking new beginnings were those suffering from the famine, poverty, and war weariness of Europe. In the fall of 1845 Fredrick Dickman, a 24 year old shoemaker and veteran of the German army, was one of the human flood of the humble who sought that new start in the young United States of America. After residing in Pennsylvania for nine years, the shoemaker moved to Hamilton County, Indiana and would enjoy a long life (81 years) full of both careers (shoemaker, farmer, woolen mill operator, store keeper and homeopathic doctor) and children (thirteen). His youngest son from his second marriage, George Conrad, would change the spelling of the family surname to Diekman, and move his young family to Henry County early in the twentieth century to start a bakery business with his brother in law.

Nicholas Van Zant grew to be a skilled wood worker, making cabinets and repairing wagons. He had a long face accentuated by his long beard and penetrating eyes. He married Sarah Ann Reed in the fall of 1854, and they had two daughters and two sons in the next seven years. The youngest son, Carl Ira, was born in September of 1861. The family lived in Liberty Township just east of New Castle.

Carl Van Zant learned the skill of wood working from his father prior to Nicholas' death when Carl was 14 years old. It is likely he used these talents to get work in one of the many saw mills in the county, or possibly in the emerging cabinet or wooden handle businesses in New Castle. At the age of 21 he married Elizabeth Katherine (Kate) Hood from the small town of Hillsboro in northern Henry County. Over the next 15 years Carl and Kate did their part to add to the rapidly growing population of the county in the post war era, having three girls and three boys. The youngest son, and fifth of six children, was named George Aaron.

New Castle was a bustling area of emerging industry with the coming of the twentieth century. Historically an agrarian and logging community, New Castle now supported such major businesses as the Hoosier Manufacturing Company (famous for the Hoosier kitchen cabinet), the Krell-French Piano Company, and the Heller Brothers Park Floral Company (famous for the development of the American Beauty Rose). Carl worked in the greenhouses that supplied award-winning roses to the nation; his young son George would ride his bike to a local bar to fill a pail with beer and bring it to his Dad and the German and Swedish immigrant co-workers at lunch. Carl also served on the New Castle Volunteer Fire Department.

The Maxwell-Briscoe automobile factory, which opened in 1907, served as a magnet to draw workers from all over to New Castle, helping to increase the once sleepy town's population over two fold during its 12 year history. Carl

Van Zant was one of those eager laborers drawn to the opportunities afforded by the Maxwell plant. He moved his family to Park Avenue, into one of the many small frame houses that grew like mushrooms around the factory.

Like his father, George Van Zant grew to be a man of modest stature. His broad face beamed, his eyes were bright and inquisitive, his lips were full, and his brown hair was closely cropped. Like his father he worked in the greenhouses, but he wanted more than the hard life of factory labor of his father and two older brothers, Frank and Charlie. Perhaps moved by his father's experience on the volunteer fire department, George sought a position with the newly formed New Castle City Fire Department, and was selected to join the company by Mayor John H. Morris in 1923. Four years later, amid local political turmoil between Democratic Mayor Strod Hayes and the city council, George Van Zant, a staunch Republican, was the surprise candidate to replace Fire Chief Victor Gilbert (whom Hayes tried to fire and ultimately resigned). It was a post he would hold through mostly Democratic city administrations for 21 years; longer than any other man in that position. He once told Democratic mayor Sydney Baker, "Syd, you're my friend and a good mayor, and I'll vote for you. But I'm a Republican, and I'll be damned if I'm voting for any other Democrat."

Marcella Mae Hessler was born and grew up on a farm near Millhousen, Indiana. Rural farm life at the turn of the century was hard. The Hessler farm was small, with a modest frame house at the end of a long dirt lane. The house had no electricity or indoor plumbing, and the land was still worked with horse drawn farm implements. The farm life held no appeal for Marcella, and she moved to New Castle in her late teens to train and work as a nurse at the Miller Hospital, just a few doors away from the Van Zant home. At some time, the tall, slender, curly haired brunette met the industrious fire fighter and, on September 29, 1924 (George's 28th birthday), at the Omer Maddox House in Knightstown, Indiana, they were married. The young couple settled in a small frame house at 2021 Lincoln Avenue, which about a year and a half later become a home for three; their first and only child Robert George arrived on April 16, 1926.

In 1935 George, Marcella and their son moved to a larger frame house at 907 S. 19th Street, with a dark brick porch on the front. On the south side of the house a driveway with a grass strip median led back to a small frame garage that sat behind the house. The house was a bit of a project, having caught fire twice in the recent past; once due to a lightning strike and once due to an alcohol still explosion in the attic. The house required lots of hammering of loose nails and many buckets of paint, but in the end it provided a most comfortable home. The ample back yard provided a wonderful playground for the young boy, allowing plenty of room for the adventures of many bands of cowboys and Indians. The security of a city government job was a blessing for the young family during the Depression. Times were tough in New Castle like everywhere else in the country. Factories producing consumer goods, like Chrysler automobiles (Chrysler bought the Maxwell-Briscoe factory in 1920), had few buyers and, as a consequence, few workers. Robert would go out on the porch on many dark mornings to find the milk box empty.

While the job of fire chief brought security, it also brought demands of considerable responsibility and danger that sometimes weighed heavily on the family. A special call box hung in the dining room at the Van Zant home that would ring whenever any of the department fire alarms sounded. George went to bed every night with a pair of rubber boots next to the nightstand. About the only time the family traveled outside the county was the one-week fishing vacation they would take in the summer. Robert lived for those trips. He loved sleeping in the cabins that sat out over the lake, listening to the waves lap gently against the sides of the fishing boats tied below. He loved spending time with his Dad. The busy Fire Chief was sometimes inaccessible; but sitting alone together in a boat in the middle of Lake George, the Fire Chief was all his. They never talked about anything too significant (the Van Zants were in general a painfully quiet lot), debating the finer points of baiting hooks and using the landing net. George would jokingly chastise his young angling companion for making so much noise he "scared every fish in the lake". Often they just sat cherishing the silence together.

The fire department was ever present. In addition to fighting over 100 fires a year (the majority house roof fires), George insured the financial, personnel, and mechanical efficiency of the department. He made annual appeals for community fire prevention awareness and safety during Fire Prevention Week each October, and reminded people of fire safety practices each Christmas season. At Christmas the fire department collected, painted and repaired, and distributed used toys to needy children. On hot summer days they would rope off a block of Main Street, and open up the fire hydrant for the benefit of the kids to play and cool off. The fire department would play the police department in charity basketball games to benefit the widows and families of those servicemen killed in the line of duty. Always on duty, George once discovered a home fire while driving to visit his parents. He caught a whiff of mysterious smoke, pulled up to the home of a Mrs. Pfleger, grabbed his chemical tank extinguisher from his Fire Chief's car, and yelled out, "Your house is on fire, lady." Upon gaining entry from Mrs. Pfleger, he ran upstairs and began working on the developing attic fire until the department pumper trucks arrived. One time when Robert was driving home late at night from a date, he turned a corner too sharply and hit a fire plug. While he was shaken but alright, he was scared at what his Dad might say about the car. As he drove up and saw the lights from the front room windows still gleaming, his heart sunk; he would have to pay the price immediately. The timid young man entered slowly, and seeing his Dad sitting in his easy chair across the room smoking his pipe, stammered out his sad story. Before he could finish his tale, George broke in impatiently asking, "Well, is the fire plug OK?"

Though he was a serious and dedicated professional, George loved a good joke. Once he came out of Engine House Number One on Church St., which sat right next to the Police Station, noticing a parking ticket on his red Chrysler Fire Chief's car, which he had temporarily parked in front of the Fire Station. The ticket cited him for illegal parking, driving without license plates, and "having his car painted in a color injurious to the eyes of the general public." He was quoted as saying that, 'while he wasn't sure if he should appear at police headquarters, he was sure the patrolman did his duty.'

George creatively responded. It seems the Police Chief George Ballard had a habit on lazy afternoons of coming over to the firehouse, sitting on the big chrome bumper of the pumper truck, and shooting the breeze. On one such afternoon, the Police Chief sauntered over and took his usual seat amongst the firemen standing around. Chief Ballard suddenly let out a yelp and leapt in the air as Chief Van Zant and the assembled firemen roared with laughter. George had taken the liberty of re-wiring the battery of the pumper truck to electrify the front bumper. The story no doubt enjoyed significant re-telling over the years, perhaps even at the wedding reception some 15 years later of George Ballard's granddaughter to George Van Zant's son.

On one occasion George was a rather unhappy recipient of a practical joke. One fall day during an election year, young Robert and his friend were riding their bikes on the busy sidewalks of downtown New Castle when they stopped to innocently inquire about the neat stickers they had at the Democratic Party Headquarters. Undoubtedly knowing a unique campaign opportunity when they saw one, the office workers happily decorated the boy's bikes with Democratic campaign stickers, and encouraged them to ride straight to the firehouse. The boys arrived at the firehouse riding their bikes that Robert described as "dressed up like circus wagons". George was standing out front talking to several people as the boys rode up with big smiles, imploring him to look at his bike. The assembled group began to chuckle as George's broad lips disappeared and his eyebrows furrowed. "Where did you get those stickers?", he grumbled.

"I got them downtown at the Democrat headquarters", Robert said proudly as the group started to now break out in laughter.

"Take that bike right home and get those stickers off," the Fire Chief demanded of the bewildered boy.

Growing up at 907 S. 19th Street was lonely. Being an only child and having a father whose work often took priority was certainly part of it, but in Robert's own words, "my family was weird."

"Dad never had much to say, and left all the correcting up to Mom. Mom was very helpful with my schoolwork, but she could be hard to please. I once asked Dad why he never got her presents for her birthday, and he said 'because anything I would get her wouldn't suit her'."

The Van Zants were not a particularly close family. Holiday gatherings occurred at Carl and Kate Van Zant's, but Robert would recall later that they seemed to lack any sense of warmth and humor. The lone exception in the dour family was his older cousin, Jeannette. She was the daughter of George's older sister Clara, who had died when Jeannette was two years old. Carl and Kate raised Jeannette, and though 17 years his senior, she served as the closest thing to a sibling that Robert knew. She would create treasure hunts at Christmas, leaving various clues around the house for the young sleuth to divine the location of his Christmas present. She took Robert on a fondly remembered road trip to Chicago to see the Museum of Natural History. Unfortunately (or fortunately perhaps) they never quite made the museum. While visiting the Indiana Dunes, the bubbly young lady thought a drive along the beach would be a great prelude to entering the city. Unbeknownst to her, Indiana beaches were nothing like the Florida beaches she had driven on, and the borrowed DeSoto she was driving quickly sunk into the loose sand dunes. While the young boy never made the museum, he did secure a toy sailboat from a Chicago dime store and successfully sailed it in Lake Michigan.

The Hesslers certainly qualified for the weird label as well in Robert's eyes. He and Marcella would visit the Hessler farm a couple of times each year, and he dreaded the boredom the weekend (usually Sunday) visits would bring. The Hesslers were devoutly Catholic, and strictly held the Sabbath as a day of rest. Robert later recalled that, "if Sunday was the only good day of weather in the whole week, they would rather the farm go to hell than them lifting a finger on Sunday." George rarely joined in the visits, making the experience even more lonely for the boy. It seems that, at least early in their marriage, Marcella's parents did not approve of her marriage "outside the faith". George Van Zant carried a protestant label but rarely attended any organized religious services. The typical visit would begin with George dropping Robert and Marcella at the end of the long dirt lane, and returning to pick them up at a pre-determined time. It wasn't until Robert was in his teens that George would accompany them for a visit, going out in the woods to hunt with Grandpa Hessler and Robert's Uncle Cressy.

The Hessler farm had gained some rusted motorized farm equipment over time, but little else had changed. Robert couldn't imagine living without electricity, and he hated having to go to the outhouse, especially in winter. His two "highlight" visits there were both bizarre and ironic. On a chilly fall day he once found a black widow spider under an old rusty bell in the back yard. When he ran into the house to tell of his discovery, his announcement was discounted by the assembled adults. Eager to prove the veracity of his claim, he went outside and using an old piece of shingle picked up the sluggishly moving spider and brought it inside the house to show the non-believers. Grandpa Hessler got up from his chair and went into the kitchen to inspect the boy's discovery and verified his claim. He then absent-mindedly placed the shingle on top of the warm cast-iron wood stove. The warm stove quickly revived the sluggish spider, and soon the adults in the living room were treated to a frantic dance of Grandpa Hessler, shoe in hand, going after the unwelcome houseguest.

The second highlight visit strangely proved to be his last. A rusted Model T Ford sat along the lane close to the house, weeds growing all around it. Seeking some recreation, he and a cousin went outside to "work on" the dilapidated vehicle. The young teenagers took wrench in hand and tried to take out the rusted spark plugs, but succeeded only in breaking the tops of each of them. Repair to the headlights resulted in a similar fate, and brought Grandpa Hessler outside with the sound of the shattering glass. It seemed that Grandpa Hessler found the boy's mechanical skills left something to be desired, and though he said nothing to Robert, he made his feelings quite clear to Marcella. She apologized and offered to pay for any damage, but it was somehow arrived at that maybe she shouldn't bring the boy down any more. Robert never had to worry about the primitive boredom of the farm again.

Robert loved tools and cars. His favorite classes in school were shop classes, and his favorite past time was drawing cars. His pictures on lined composition paper had compass rendered wheels, covered by gracefully flowing fenders. As he got older, he naturally joined his loves into working on cars. Sometimes passion exceeded wisdom however. As a surprise for his father one day, Robert changed the spark plugs on the family sedan. Upon completion when Robert started the car it gave out a most horrible groan and rumble and the motor shook "like it was trying to jump out of the car". Upon calling his Dad he discovered for the first time that spark plug wires had to be returned in a particular order. Defying George's orders to leave the car alone till he got home, the industrious novice mechanic went over to the neighbor's car, which was also a Chevy V-6, opened the hood, and made a diagram of the spark plug wire placement. The Chevy was purring once again by the time George got home, but Robert got a lecture on respecting the privacy of other people's property. His love of cars would follow him into adulthood, making him the proud owner and primary mechanic of over 30 vehicles, from a 1936 Dodge to a 1999 Buick.

The events of Sunday, December 7th, 1941 would change the entire world, and 907 S.19th Street was not immune. The Van Zants learned of the bombing of Pearl Harbor like many people; listening to shocking news reports on their large cabinet radio. A sophomore in high school, Robert probably thought little about how such events half way around the world might affect him. He was more concerned about getting through Latin class and looking forward to getting his first driver's license. Over the course of his high school days, though full of normal events like attending basketball games, dating, and running around with his friends, his thoughts had to wonder across the seas. As graduation approached in May, 1944, he knew he would likely see the end of that year in some location far distant from New Castle, Indiana.

Private Robert G. Van Zant, US Army, January, 1945.

The first fall breezes of September gently rustled the leaves of the trees surrounding the courthouse, and created crisp sounding ripples in the 48 star flag that flew from the tall pole in front of the courthouse steps. The Civil War era bronze soldier stood silent sentry over the lone bus parked on Main Street in front of the stately brick and stone building. Gradually cars began to arrive, and a growing crowd began to congregate. A line of young men dressed in slacks, buttoned shirts, and light jackets that were all carrying small suitcases, began to form in front of the bus.

"Dad took me to the courthouse. I got on the bus, and as it pulled out I waved goodbye." In a scene that was played out everyday in most every town in America in the fall of 1944, Robert Van Zant, an 18 year-old boy who just graduated from high school four months before, was about to join the active ranks of what would later be described as "The Greatest Generation", facing what would be their greatest test; global warfare.

"Like everybody else, I was eager to go to war. I wanted to get into the Navy. I had read Ernie Pyle's articles about the life of an infantryman, and I preferred sleeping in a bunk of a ship instead of a water-filled hole someplace. When I was called up though, the Navy quota had already been reached, so I was in the Army."

His bus ride ended at Camp Atterbury, just south of Indianapolis, where he was issued his uniform. Not long after that, he was on a train headed for basic training at Camp Fannin in Tyler, Texas. For a kid who had never traveled any further than the states bordering Indiana, this was the first step of what would be an amazing journey.

"It seemed like it rained every day there. There were rivers and lakes of red Texas mud everywhere. Our company started out under First Sergeant Tribby. He was a short guy but a sharp dresser; always looked like he just stepped out of a magazine. He had us first in everything. We then lost Sergeant Tribby, and then got some hillbilly sergeant from Alabama and went from being first to being last in everything. This bugged the sergeant to the point that one night before falling out, he told us that 'I don't care what it takes, I want you guys on the parade ground first tomorrow.' Well, the next morning at reveille, we stormed out of the barracks doors. The only problem was the doors opened in and we ran right through the screens; but we were first on the parade grounds. That hillbilly sergeant was burning up, but he couldn't say nothing 'cause he told us to do whatever it took to get there first."

"Basic training was mostly marching everywhere carrying an M1 rifle. We bivouacked in the rain. I got my picture in the paper out on bivouac. Some photographer was going around the camp and called for someone to stick their head out for a picture and 'show us a big Pepsodent smile.' I sent the picture back to the folks. We did some target practice. I was a good shot for me; no more practice than I had before then. The only time I shot a rifle was hunting down in Westport or practicing with Dad's .22 down in the basement. He'd put a target in the fruit room, and I'd stand at the bottom of the stairs and shoot."

Once he completed basic training, he was on a train returning to New Castle for a ten-day furlough. He 'hung out in the Chevy mostly' and got pictures taken in his uniform. After the all too brief furlough, he was off to Fort Ord in California, where he would begin a gypsy migration through a series of replacement camps before his eventual departure to the Pacific theater. Back home, Marcella hung a blue star banner in the front window of their home on South 19th Street; a reminder to the neighborhood of her son's service.

"The group ahead of us at Camp Fannin went straight to Europe and the Battle of the Bulge. We all would have rather gone to Europe. It was going to be over quicker, and I had visions of these awful jungles that were hot and humid. Besides, the Germans had sense enough to surrender, but the Japanese you had to shoot. It's kinda' scary when you know the guy you're fighting doesn't care about dying."

After two weeks at Fort Ord, he was sent to Fort Lawton in Washington. More waiting and marching to endure.

"I got in with a couple of guys from Dayton, Ohio. One was a Jewish guy who was an expert at goofing off. We were marching on the parade ground one day, and he said 'When the platoon gets over the hill, let's just make a right and march over to the PX.' Every day after that, the sergeant marched right along side us. Marching was boring. I'd spend most of my time looking at cars when we were marching."

The end of February saw the young private board a Liberty ship headed for Hawaii. This was considerably different than navigating the waters of Lake George in a fishing boat.

"The trip from Washington to Hawaii was rough. I was fighting seasickness a lot. I was OK as long as I could be on deck, but once I was below deck, I'd feel sick."

"Once we got to Oahu, we took a narrow gauge train to our camp. We spent about a month here, and got some jungle training. From Hawaii we were sent to Saipan, spending about two or three weeks there. We weren't sure where we would be going; China, Taiwan, or Okinawa. We knew where we were going to end up though; Japan."

"We set off from Saipan in a big convoy. We weren't allowed to sleep on deck out of Saipan, and I still got sick being below deck. A buddy and I figured a way to get on deck to sleep though. We would tie our ponchos around our waist under our coats, and then tell the guy guarding the door we were going on deck for a smoke. Once on deck we would sneak under a landing tank, snap our ponchos together, and go to sleep. You had to be sure to get well under the tank, cause the guards on deck would come around and poke their night sticks under the edges of the tank."

Not long after marking his 19th birthday somewhere on the Pacific, the odyssey that began from New Castle, Indiana eight months before, ended on the other side of the world as Robert disembarked from a landing craft onto a floating dock extending out from an Okinawan beach.

"We landed not long after the initial landing, so the beach was secured. It wasn't too bad after that first night. I was really scared that first night. You always worried about infiltrators. Anything you saw on the other side of the line you shot."

Robert Van Zant was assigned to the 96th Division, 381st Battalion, B Company; serial number 35108789. The 96th Division was involved in the thrust to the southern end of the island to conquer the primary Japanese resistance. He soon adapted to the daily routine of the campaign.

"You would have a morning objective, you would make it, and usually stopped in the late afternoon (right around martini time), and dug in for the night. It rained every damn day in May, and so you usually spent your night in a fox hole full of water. The mosquitoes were terrible. Once you were dug in, they would bring up water in five gallon Jerry cans. We ate C rations, some with pre-World War I dates, with beans, veggies, and spam. It was tough sleeping in a wet fox hole, but if you got tired enough, you would sleep."

"One night I was so sick and tired of being dirty and grimy, I took a whole Jerry can of water back to my little tent and, using my helmet, had a wash, shave, and brushed my teeth. I had to dig a slit trench for taking the water, but I sure felt better taking a bath."

He spent two to three months on the line. The daily routine was anything but routine however. The daily objective might be over rice paddies or through mountains pock-marked with caves.

"We would start out with a squad taking the point. A different squad took the point each day. We might march right up to a cliff full of caves and not have a shot fired at us. One day the squad out on point came under fire. Only two guys made it back to our lines the next morning."

"One day our squad was on point, and we came under fire. The sergeant wanted somebody to go back to our lines and tell the commander we needed help. I wasn't too happy about being chosen to go back, but then I wasn't too

31

happy staying at the front and being shot at either. As I ran back to the line, I tripped and fell down about two or three times. In basic we were trained to fall down when running in the open as an evasive technique, but this was just me tripping over my own feet. When I got back, the sergeant complimented me on my evasive technique. I didn't have the heart to tell him I was just real good at tripping over my own feet."

"We came across very few villages; most had been flattened by artillery or bombing. Whenever you came across a rice paddy, you would spread out and wade through it instead of walking on the paths around it. It was for safety and speed. You didn't want to bunch up and be an inviting target for mortars or artillery. The GI hated artillery; at least the enemies' artillery. I remember crouching down in a foxhole, shells whistling over my head, and saying a lot of Hail Mary's. Every time I say it now, I think about that."

"About half way through me being on the line, I became a BAR (Browning Automatic Rifle) man. I got this BAR from a guy who had been shot. Our sergeant said, 'Van Zant, you're a big guy, you're our BAR man. The BAR was about twice as heavy as an M1, but it shot 20 rounds continuously. The M1 had an eight round clip, single shot. The BAR had been in this rice paddy for days. When I first pulled the trigger, mud flew out the barrel and it fired really slow. I was cleaning rust off it constantly, but I got it cleaned up to the point it could fire."

"Every night when we dug in, we would tie trip wires with ration cans and hand grenades in front of our lines to prevent infiltrators. I remember one night I thought I saw a shadow and opened up; tracer bullets flying out into the night from that BAR. Next morning we went out to look around, but nothing was there."

"The civilians hid in the caves, and came out at night to look for food, but the Jap soldiers also roamed at night. One night we heard noise beyond the line, and we opened up. In the morning we went out and found a civilian family of a beautiful young girl, an old man and women, and a boy. The boy was shot in the jaw, and the girl had a splint on her arm from some previous injury, and the arm was yellow and green. They were scared because the Japanese had told them we were going to kill and rape them all. We yelled for a medic, stacked our guns up, and slowly walked over to them. I took out a chocolate bar, and offered it to the girl. She wouldn't take it at first, so I took a bite, and then gave it to her again and she finally took it. Me and another GI crossed our hands and began carrying the old women back to our lines. She grabbed a hold of my arms and wouldn't let go. By the time we got back to our lines, we were friends…or at least she wasn't scared of us."

The 96th was involved in mop-up operations in the south end of the island, attempting to dislodge the last vestige of the defiant Japanese forces.

"We would blow up caves and try to get prisoners if we could. We were so glad to have the best artillery and mortars; it sure made our lives easier. We were the best-equipped army on Earth. In going into those caves, we were glad to have flame throwers; though I often thought what a terrible death that would be."

As mop-up operations came to a close and Okinawa was secured, Robert found his way to a rest area to await the next move.

"We figured we were next going into China and Japan after that. In the rest area, there was an opening for two cooks, and this guy from North Carolina talked me into it. He thought that if we were cooks, wherever we went next we wouldn't be up on the front lines. Outside of having to get up at the crack of dawn, it wasn't a bad job. One day we were fixing lemonade for lunch, and I started pouring water out of this Jerry can into the powder mix when I heard a sergeant yell at me, 'Don't pour that in there! You want to get the whole camp drunk!' Instead of water, I had started to pour their home brew alcohol, what they called 'torpedo juice', into the mix."

His next move would not be China or Japan, but back towards home.

"I was shot in the rest area. I was sitting in our tent writing a letter. The sergeant kept a souvenir revolver, and the guys were always coming in and playing with it. He always kept the first chamber empty. One guy came in and picked it up; it clicked once and then it went off. I felt something graze my knee, then a burning in my right palm and little finger. I turned to him and said, 'You shot me!' My whole hand started to burn, and we got the medic. He got me to the hospital."

"The first question they asked me was 'Did you shoot yourself?' I said 'No, my best friend shot me.' The nurse said 'You need to get a new best friend.' They performed surgery there to remove the bullet, and put me in a cast with pins to stabilize it and a rubber band to hold my finger out."

He was flown to a Navy hospital in Guam, where he heard about the atomic bombs dropped on Hiroshima and Nagasaki. A few days later, via Armed Forces Radio, he listened as World War II came to an end on the deck of the USS Missouri.

The remainder of 1945 and early 1946 was filled with more surgery and rehabilitation at Fletcher General Hospital in Cambridge, Ohio and Cushing General Hospital in Framingham, Massachusetts. While at Fletcher General, he would frequently make it home for weekends, hitchhiking across Ohio and back again. His last post was Fort Sheridan, Illinois from which he was formally honorably discharged from the Army on July 31, 1946. He returned to New Castle, glad to be home and itching to get behind the wheel of an automobile. Marcella removed the blue star banner from the window with a sense of relief, carefully rolled it up, and reverently placed it in the bedroom chest of drawers, along with a leather bound folder with clippings she had taken from the local newspaper for the past two years that had chronicled her son's service.

When he returned home, he was like many of the returning young veterans; excited to start living and anxious to put the war behind them. He would be like any other guy of the post-war era; worker, homeowner, consumer, parent to baby boomers. But in those brief two years, both he and the world would be forever changed. His was but one of 16 million different American stories of the conflict that ultimately defined his time. But his story also defined who he became, and how he would pass through life.

SILENCING A SMILE

The Carl Van Zant Family, New Castle, Indiana, circa 1905.
Left to Right; Frank, Alice, Carl, Clara, Kate, George, Charlie

When you look at the faded family photograph from the early 1900's, you are automatically drawn to the smile. The young teenage girl sitting on the top step of the wooden porch has a beaming smile that lights up her pretty face. Her long dark hair is pulled back and tied up loosely on top of her head. Between her parents who are sitting in wooden rocking chairs, both with rather dour expressions, she creates a stark contrast of demeanor. Her older twin brothers stand on either side of the steps, one sporting a bowler hat and the other a cap, each exhibiting rather cocksure expressions. Her younger brother sits one step below her, hair tousled and smiling. Her young sister sits on the bottom step, her long hair tied in a bow almost as big as her head, with a somewhat bewildered look on her face. Hanging ferns decorate the porch of the wood frame house. It all seems quite typical for the conservative Victorian era, and yet the smile seems oddly out of place. It is bright, cheerful, inviting, and perhaps even a little dangerous.

Clara Van Zant was a mystery, both in life and death. Hers was a short life, passionately lived and, tragically, passionately ended. She was the third child born to Carl and Kate Van Zant, arriving January 16, 1894. She must have been a happy, fun loving child. She must have embraced life, and sought all the wonder it could offer. This was probably much to the chagrin of her parents, themselves quiet and reserved working class people from pioneer families in the county. But Clara must have been touched by a special gift (or curse) to live outside the mold.

By the age of 15, the vibrant Clara, seemingly in stark contrast to her independent nature, found herself a bride. On May 29, 1909 she married 19 year-old Jesse Freel. Freel, the son of the county engineer William Freel, was tall and lean, with fair-complected skin and closely cut dark hair. His ears stuck out wide from his head, and his thick eyebrows failed only slightly from meeting in the center of his prominent forehead. Following the wedding, the couple moved into the Freel family home. Exactly six months later, on November 29, 1909, Clara became a mother with the birth of her daughter

Jeannette. The consequences, blessed though they were, had caught up with her.

Kate, who had not visited her daughter at the Freel's home since the wedding, went over to help her daughter with the baby. Eventually the teenage parents were able to move into a small house on Webster Avenue in May of 1910, but they found they were ill prepared for their new life. Two months later Jesse deserted the family unexpectedly, and Clara and Jeannette had to move in with her parents. Clara got a job working as a telephone operator at the Maxwell-Briscoe automobile factory. Carl and Kate enjoyed their granddaughter, and began proceedings to formally adopt young Jeannette. They saw the same joy, innocence, and precocious nature in her face that they remembered in Clara.

On her 17th birthday, Clara was back in the loving arms of her family, working to support her beautiful one year-old daughter, and realizing that she needed to get back to forging a new path for her life and that of her daughter.

One year after leaving his family, Jesse Freel resurfaced in New Castle in July of 1911, apparently seeking reconciliation with his young bride and daughter. Clara was convinced however that she and Jeannette needed to move on, and not long after Freel's return, she wrote a letter to her husband seeking a divorce:

> Jesse,
>
> After our conversation last night, I have come to the
> conclusion that the best thing for me to do is to get a
> divorce, being the best for all concerned. I find that I do
> not love you as a wife should a husband, and never can.
> Perhaps I made some mistakes in my married life, but
> if I did so it was through ignorance as I was too young
> to realize. I intend to get the divorce and, of course, the

custody of Jeannette. You can come and see her whenever you want to, and take her away at times; also your folks can have and see her whenever you want to. I think I should have custody as my folks cared for her when nobody else would and have grown to love her dearly. It would be wrong to take her away from them now. If I don't get the custody of Jeannette you know what will happen to me within two weeks as she is all I have and I can not live without her.

Clara

Clara began, quite publicly, seeking a new life. She was seen around town with friends, both male and female, at dances, parties, and strolls in the park. This behavior was thought by some unseemly, and the police reportedly instructed her to "cease becoming so conspicuous". It is unlikely the dismissive views of a nosey community and constabulary were going to stop Clara from exploring a renewed zest for life.

Freel, described as "a man of peculiar make up hardly understood even by his own relatives", was making no mystery of his feelings regarding the impending demise of his marriage and his bride's actions. He reportedly wrote her letters seeking reconciliation while at the same time threatening her life. To Clara's young brother George, Freel indicated that he intended to try to get her to live with him again, and if she refused, "he would fix it so she would not go with anyone else". He further told George that, "I am not afraid of the electric chair, the gallows, or anything else." Freel was seen following Clara around town, hanging around the Van Zant home late at night, and even following the family on a train trip to Sandusky. He made similar threats to Clara's young sister Alice as well. On the whole however, the Van Zant family took little stock in Freel's threats; considering them only empty talk from a distraught and confused young man.

Freel was known to carry a revolver regularly. He had shown it to the Van Zant boys before he left Clara and Jeannette. He came over to the Van Zant home late on July 4th, and shot the gun six times before Kate chased him off. There were even stories that he had threatened suicide during their marriage, going off in the woods and discharging the weapon. To his friends Freel spoke constantly of his wife's conduct and "getting the men running after her".

In August at a five-cent dance at the Moose Lodge, Clara was introduced to a handsome 21 year-old man named Ralph Hunter. Hunter worked at the Miller Grocery, and had a reputation as a "bad actor who led a sinful life of forcing his attentions on young (and sometimes married) women." The temptations on several levels were probably too much for the "merry widow" (as some were referring to Clara) to decline. Hunter would frequently meet and talk to Clara as she walked to work. She and Hunter would periodically see each other in the company of friends. In addition to public dances and ball games there were walks along Maxwell Park at night. The public relationship was becoming private as well.

One late September evening Clara, Ralph, and Clara's friend Winnie Pritchett spent the evening down at the school, drinking and reading from a book of Hunter's that contained "obscene poetry". Later that evening, Jesse came upon the scene and was enraged. He vigorously grabbed Clara by the arm and pulled her away from the intimate group, demanding to know what she was doing with Hunter. A brief, passionate argument ensued, as Hunter and Pritchett slowly moved away toward the schoolhouse steps. Clara violently jerked her arm away from Jesse, and quickly moved toward her friends, all the while giving Jesse a cold and disparaging glance over her shoulder. She went up to Hunter, placed both her hands on his cheeks, slowly pulled his lips to hers and kissed him. An astonished Freel turned and ran away.

A few weeks later, Jesse approached Hunter at the train station, and calmly asked that, as a favor to him to leave Clara alone, as he was trying to secure a divorce, and if he would leave her alone, she would comply. Hunter agreed that he would.

On Sunday, October 8th, Clara and some friends attended a ball game at Maxwell Park, and met Ralph Hunter there. The small group got together after the game, and walked away under the watchful eye of Jesse Freel. Later Freel went down to the Honey Bee Cigar Store and Pool Hall at the corner of 12th and Broad Streets. An enraged Freel spoke of "his slut of a wife and all the wolves running after her" as he rocketed the cue ball toward the racked balls at the end of the table, and stared angrily as they exploded in all directions.

The evening of Friday, October 13th was cool and clear. Carl Van Zant and his son Frank were working the late shift at the Maxwell-Briscoe factory. Kate, after helping Clara get Jeannette to bed, started back to the kitchen to finish preparing dinner for Carl and Frank when they arrived home later. Clara was going down to the station to meet William Moore, a friend from work, due in from Detroit on the 7:30 pm train. Wearing a white waist shirt under a red sweater and blue shirt, she made her way to the door while putting on a heavier red sweater. Calling goodbye as she opened the screen door, she left her home for the last time.

Clara had met her friend Bessie Burris at the station, and they talked while waiting for the train. Ralph Hunter arrived at the station later, and the three talked as the 7:30 train arrived. William Moore was not on the train however, and so Clara and Bessie decided to mill about on Broad Street while Ralph took care of an errand, and they made arrangements to meet on 15th Street at 9:00 pm.

Jesse Freel exited the Honey Bee Cigar Store around 8:50 pm and commenced walking east toward the train station. After walking two blocks he noticed Clara and another woman across the street about a block away standing under the halo of light produced by the gas light street lamps. Before long he noticed another figure approach. As the face appeared out of the shadows and entered the light he recognized Ralph Hunter. His blood ran hot as he stepped in the shadows and breathed heavily as he watched the trio walk away.

After walking Bessie Burris home, Ralph and Clara sauntered toward the Van Zant home, completely unaware of the figure that followed them away off in the shadows. Arriving in the front of the home a little after 10:00 pm, Clara and Ralph continued their conversation, Ralph sitting atop a wooden fence while Clara leaned next to one of the fence posts. Hidden off in the blackness west of the house, Freel listened intently. While he could not make out much of the conversation, the lilt of Clara's laugh traveled hauntingly through the night air. His grip on the .38 caliber revolver tightened so that his knuckles were white as marble, and without thought withdrew the weapon from his coat pocket and stormed out of the darkness toward the couple next to the fence, dimly lit by the gas light lamp.

"Hunter, what in the hell are you doing here?", Freel demanded, and without warning raised the pistol and shot Hunter before he knew what was happening. Hunter, hit in the left arm, staggered off the fence as Clara let out a terrified scream. Freel turned toward Clara and, from less than three inches away, shot her in the back, the bullet traveling upward and into her left lung. She collapsed to the ground, still screaming though less forcefully.

Hunter had gained his feet under him, and began to run north when Freel turned toward him and rapidly fired two more shots, bringing down his fleeing target with wounds to the back and left chest. With Hunter prostrate on the ground, he fired once more into the victim's left groin.

Carl and Frank Van Zant had returned from a long shift at the factory at about 9:30 pm, and had just finished up dinner. Frank went straight to bed, and Carl went to the dimly lit living room and fell into the armchair to scan the day's *Daily Courier*. The loud crack of the revolver made him jump, and he charged to the back door to find only blackness. The shots and the screams he knew to be his daughter's kept coming, and he ran through the house to the front door. At that same moment Kate came running down the steps, hurriedly slipping on her housecoat over her dressing gown, a desperate look of confusion and fear on her face.

Carl threw the front door open and charged out onto the porch with Kate in rapid pursuit. He knocked over one of the ferns as he bounded down the porch steps, and focused on the two figures in the dim lamp light. His daughter was lying in a crumpled mass on her stomach and right side, her head turned to the left. Jesse Freel stood over her, revolver in his right hand, staring at his wife as she continued to let loose a gurgling, weakening scream.

Kate screamed from behind him, "Please God, stop the shooting!", as Carl began down the walk toward the pair. He saw Freel slowly place the gun to the back of Clara's head and, in a moment of terror that seemed like an eternity, he saw a flash of light from the muzzle of the gun, and heard a loud crack as he saw his daughter's head recoil and heard the deafening silence of the screams that were no more.

"Freel, you son of a bitch, I'll get you for this", Carl screamed as he ran towards Freel with his arms outstretched as if he were chocking the very air in front of him. Freel briefly looked up at the approaching Carl, then turned and ran west into the darkness.

Carl watched as Freel vanished into the blackness, and then turned and knelt next to Clara. Though repulsed by the sight, he cupped his hand around the mass of scattered bone, blood, and brain that was now the back of her head, rolled her to her back, placed his other hand under her knees, and picked her up as the distraught Kate arrived on the scene. Sobbing uncontrollably, Kate followed her husband to the house and opened the door for him as he carried Clara into the house. Neither of them heard the cries from the darkness pleading, "For God's sake, some one come here and help me."

The Van Zant boys had assembled in the living room as Carl gently laid Clara on the sofa. He slowly stepped away and briefly stared at her beautiful young face. Blood now slowly flowed from her mouth and nose as Kate cried while gently blotting the trails of blood and softly stroking Clara's hair out of her face. Her shallow breathing made a gurgling sound. He knew her life was leaving her.

Carl told Frank and Charlie to call the doctor and the police. Kate quietly told George to go upstairs and stay with Alice and Jeannette, and not let them come downstairs. Doctor J. Gronendyke was quickly called, but he declined treatment unless he was guaranteed payment. A second physician declined to "get involved in the murders". Finally, a borrowed buggy was secured, and Carl and Kate transported Clara to Butler Hospital, arriving at 11:30 pm and where, about an hour later, they were informed by Dr. Koons of the death of their oldest daughter.

The police had arrived at the Van Zant home and placed the injured Ralph Hunter in a buggy, transporting him to Dr. Gronendyke who once again denied treating the party without payment. Ultimately Hunter found his way to Butler Hospital as well, where Dr. Koons removed the bullet from his chest. The bullets in the arm and groin could not be immediately located, and X-rays showed the bullet in the back had lodged next to a spinal disk. Hunter was experiencing paralysis in his legs.

After fleeing into the night, Freel found himself at his familiar haunt, The Honey Bee. Though sweating and out-of-breath, he settled himself into a well-worn straight back wooden chair. He felt a multitude of eyes peering through the smoky air and settling on his form. The stillness grew eerily disturbing, until he broke it saying matter-of-factly, "Well, I just killed my wife and the son of a bitch that was with her." The dumbfounded gathering looked on in silence, until the gravity of events began to settle upon the young Freel. He slowly shook his head, and then buried it into his hands.

Carl and Kate walked up the blood stained walk, past the de-potted fern, and into their living room. A policeman said they had done all they could tonight, and would return in the morning to investigate the crime scene. Upon extending his condolences for their loss, he departed. The three boys were sitting in the dining room, heavy with confusion and sorrow. Both Alice and Jeannette had fallen back to sleep. Carl fell into the armchair, and stared at the blood-stained sofa that had served as Clara's final resting place in their home. Memories came flooding over him in torrents. It was all he could do to not betray his overwhelming sense of loss. As Kate, sitting next to him, started once again to cry uncontrollably, he got up and knelt next to her, softly accepting her head on his shoulder.

After collecting himself, Freel calmly walked out of the Honey Bee and down to the Police station. Upon entering, he immediately sought out his friend Sam Ives. He held out his arms in front of Policeman Ives and said, "Sam, put the cuffs on. I just killed Clara and Ralph Hunter."

"I was just gonna start out looking for you," he responded as he complied with Freel's request. Ives went through Freel's pockets, retrieving the .38 revolver and several shells.

Freel then asked to call his mother and, before being led to a cell, remarked off-handedly, "Sam, I want to register. I've never stayed in a hotel where I haven't registered."

The banner headline of the Saturday *Daily Courier* blared "Jesse Freel Kills Wife and Wounds her Lover". The police had come to the Van Zant home in the morning to investigate the crime scene. In addition to interviewing Carl and Kate, they found three spent .38 caliber shell casings. Early in the morning, Carl had made arrangements with the undertaker. Clara's funeral would be in their living room on Monday. That evening the William Freel family stopped to express their sympathies and to submit a strange request from their son. It seems after seeing Jesse in jail that morning, he requested release from jail to "attend the funeral of my wife."

No doubt holding back his anger as well as his shock at the audacity of the request, he replied to the Freels and the state authorities saying, "I may not be able to control myself. It is best he stay away. My daughter, though wayward, was dear to me, and I can't but hold the deepest hatred for the man who caused her death. She is dead, but God knows she is better off than the man who ended her life."

Freel learned of Carl Van Zant's response to his request Sunday, and was likely not surprised. His parents had brought his guitar to the jail, and he had spent most of the day playing popular airs on his guitar. It is reported his favorite was "A Boy's Best Friend is His Mother."

An outpouring of sympathy came from family, friends, and the community. Flowers and mourners (including Mr. and Mrs. William Freel) filled the Van Zant home on Monday, October 16th, as the Reverend L.C. Howe of Noblesville (formerly the pastor of the New Castle Christian Church) officiated at Clara's funeral. No mention was made regarding the method of her passing, but Reverend Howe exhorted those gathered to "lead a life of uprightness and purity."

On Wednesday, October 25th a grand jury, after hearing testimony from almost 50 witnesses (including the Van Zant family), handed down an indictment for first-degree murder against Jesse Freel. Upon hearing the indictment, Freel nonchalantly asked when the trial would be, and went about tuning his guitar. Asked if he thought he was in a serious predicament, Freel responded, "Oh, not very."

On Tuesday, February 20, 1912, a recovering Ralph Hunter arrived at the train station from his home in Cloverdale to prepare to testify for the trial to begin on Thursday. The paralysis he had experienced after the incident had slowly subsided, until he was able to go home to Cloverdale in mid-November. Hunter was now able to walk without the aid of crutches, but his gait was stiff and he was in near constant pain. The prosecuting team, consisting of head prosecutor H.H. Evans, deputy prosecutor C.E. DeWitt, and counsel retained by the Van Zant family, James H. Jones, would call 38 witnesses in its case against Freel. A total of 15 witnesses were slated to testify for the defense team of W.C. Barnard, W.E. Jeffery, and F.C. Gause.

Thursday morning's session began with jury selection. Under the watchful eye of Judge Edward Jackson, the prosecution and defense dispensed of a total of 29 potential jurors before a final jury of 12 was impaneled. All those selected indicated they had no reservations against administration of the death penalty. The defendant sat quietly, looking pale with dark circles under his eyes.

By the time of the opening statements the court gallery was filled, with people standing along the back wall of the room. Following the statements for the prosecution and defense, the state called Ralph Hunter to the stand. Hunter stiffly approached the witness chair, slowly lowering himself and tucking his knees under his chin, as this was the only position in which he could sit without extreme pain. Under prosecution questions, Hunter recounted the events of October 13th in graphic detail. Kate Van Zant frequently broke down, weeping quietly onto Carl's shoulder. Freel seemed to focus intently on the questioning. The prosecution's questioning of Hunter concluded Thursday's session, with cross-examination of Hunter slated to open Friday's session. Judge Jackson cautioned the jury not to discuss the case, but declined to sequester the jury.

People formed a line outside the locked courtroom as early as 6:00 am Friday morning to ensure being seated in the gallery. Judge Jackson refused scores of people seeking admission into the court, as Hunter took the stand once more. In cross-examination the defense sought to portray Hunter as the aggressor that night, seeking to attack Freel who acted initially then in self-defense and, only as a result of that rage, killed his wife. Hunter was not swayed in his testimony however, holding strong to his conviction that he and Clara were the victims of an unprovoked attack.

Following testimony of Policeman Ives and several neighbors recounting what they heard that night, the prosecution called Kate Van Zant to the stand. Kate testified regarding the history of Clara and Jesse's relationship, and his actions since his return to town last July. She was then asked to recount the events of the night of the killing. She sobbed uncontrollably as the prosecution asked her to identify Clara's blood stained clothes. Carl was then asked to testify to his account of that night. As reported at the time, he "mastered his compassions and controlled himself from start to finish" during his testimony. The 16 year-old George Van Zant was the last witness called prior to the 12:30 pm recess. George recounted his exchanges with Freel since his return to town, indicating he had threatened Clara's life and was constantly following her every move.

At 3:30 pm, following a brief discussion with counsel at his bench, Judge Jackson stunned the crowd when he asked the accused to stand and announced, "It is the understanding of the court you wish to change your plea from not guilty to guilty of murder in the second degree. Are you guilty or not guilty?"

Freel, head bowed, responded in a voice audible to the judge and some of the jury, "guilty." A collective buzz immediately rose from the gallery that was quickly silenced with Judge Jackson's gavel.

"I find you guilty of murder in the second degree," Judge Jackson pronounced, "and I sentence you to life imprisonment at the state penitentiary in Michigan City." He then paused briefly and looked Freel in the eye. "How old are you?"

"I am 23," Freel responded as a tear slowly made its way down his right cheek. He was immediately led out of the courtroom and to the jail, there to await transport to Michigan City the next day.

It seems that defense counsel over the long recess discussed the plea agreement with the Freel family and approached the prosecution with the offer. James Jones, attorney for the Van Zant family, faithfully executed Kate's desire to reject the plea, but ultimately was convinced to accept it. They figured the jury would likely return a similar verdict and, if not, Governor Marshall had gone on public record stating "no person shall be legally executed during my term in office."

Freel boarded a train for Michigan City at 5:00 pm Saturday, accompanied by Henry County Sheriff Kirk. According to Kirk, Freel was "light-hearted and gay" on the ride to prison. He said he never meant to kill Clara, and that he prayed for Hunter's recovery. He hoped that he would secure a pardon or parole in the future. Kirk also related that Freel made at least two attempts to escape while in jail in New Castle. In one case, Freel and his friend Sherman French had cooked up a plan in which French would smuggle saws into the jail by getting drunk in public and getting arrested. French did get drunk, but apparently failed to follow through on the remainder of the assignment.

Freel was initially assigned to a bookkeeping job at the penitentiary, due to his adeptness with figures as a result of his experience as an engineer's assistant. Freel worked under the Reverand William E. Hinshaw, a former Methodist preacher, serving a life sentence for the murder of his wife. Freel later worked also in the mail office and the hospital, but he spent most of his time working in "the yard". Freel's sentence was commuted to 20 years on July 30, 1928 by Indiana Governor Edward L. Jackson; the same man who, as judge in New Castle, had proclaimed his life sentence 16 years earlier. Freel would not live to enjoy this reprieve however, dying in prison following a brief illness on July 12, 1930.

Carl and Kate Van Zant planted peony bushes around the white gravestone of Clara Freel. They raised Jeannette Freel Van Zant as their daughter. The young girl was bright, happy, and precocious; undoubtedly a happy yet haunting reflection of her mother. As a young women she dated, but could never find someone that pleased either her or Carl and Kate. She ultimately never married, living with a female companion most of her life. She maintained contact with her father's family throughout her life. She was always the favorite relative of Robert Van Zant, the only "fun and normal" relative he recalled from childhood. They remained close until Jeannette's death from brain cancer on June 19, 1971. When Robert and George Van Zant went down to Florida to settle Jeannette's affairs, they were surprised to learn that her estate had been left to a male friend, with only family items marked for both the Van Zant and Freel families withheld from the general estate.

The events of October 13, 1911 were never discussed in the Van Zant household, at least not above a respectable whisper. Robert never learned of the events surrounding the death of Jeannette's mother until the parents of a girl he was dating in high school told him the story. Robert also recalls his Dad receiving frequent phone calls from the local bar owners asking George to "come and pick up your Dad; he's tied a big one on again." It seems Carl later made a practice of cashing his payroll check at the bars that surrounded the factory, and frequently spent the night and early morning drinking. Perhaps attempting to drown the demons surrounding the images of that October night.

The picture is almost a century old now, and the images, as well as the lives to which they were linked, are beginning to be lost to the fading of time. Yet there is still something alluring about the smile. Though silenced so long ago, it calls from the ages, relating the story of a life; happy, exciting and tragic.

Carl Diekman, 17 year-old traveler, in Long Beach, California, 1919.

Everyone had settled in. Uncle Bud stretched his long legs out from Grandpa's over-stuffed, sky blue easy chair. My Mom sat to his right in the other easy chair, with my Dad sitting to her right on the couch. Ensconced in other seats about the room were Aunt Marion and her son Gary Rhodes, and Aunt Dot and her son Marty Ballard. Baskets of flowers of every shape, color, and size were scattered hither and thither on the wooden floor. My cousins Margo and Carla and my brother were in the dining room behind the living room, going through old photographs and papers scattered haphazardly on the rectangular walnut table. Conversations filled the air in both rooms, recounting memories of both the recent and distant past, becoming a verbal vortex to my ears.

As I had when I was a kid, I took the opportunity to slip away under the cover of conversation, and made my way through the tiny kitchen to the stairs that descended into the basement. Five steps took you to the landing of the side door, and off to the left was the stairway to the basement. It was a narrow stairwell with cold concrete walls painted battleship grey. An old pipe banister ran along the right side as you walked down the ten concrete steps, worn smooth with use.

The large open basement ran the length of the house below the dining room and living room, and the early afternoon light was shining through the windows on the north and east sides of the main room. It created enough light to see the large clear light bulb hanging from the white ceramic fixture attached to the living room floor joist. I pulled the long white cord now grimy from years of use, and the curly element in the bulb began to glow, giving light to the main display area. The south half of the basement had for years been, to me, a museum. It was here my grandfather had assembled the various treasures and trinkets from his travels. A rickety series of shelves ran the length of the south wall, crammed with books, magazines, bottles, jars, glasses, rocks, cigar boxes, and a veritable cornucopia of the odd and bizarre. I spent uncounted hours of my childhood wondering, as the adult conversations seeped through the floorboards, about the stories behind each of the oddities I found, held, and closely inspected.

I walked over to the east wall where the "travel table" sat. This was a small rectangular coffee table that, below its glass top, Grandpa had placed matchbook covers from various places across the country. Hotels, motels, restaurants, gas stations, and tourist traps were all represented. He and Grandma had made a point of car traveling when they were a young married couple. Even though he worked incredibly hard at making his bakery a successful small business during the depths of the Depression, he and Marie always took a week off in the summer. They would have one of Marie's sisters come down to sit with the kids, and they would climb in the car, sometimes with a plan but sometimes not, and drive. Upon their return, a plate from their destination found its way up on the display rail that circled the dining room. By the time they had stopped their travels, they had most all the states of the union represented. The travel table was a microcosm of those legendary excursions, remembering times of auto travel before the super highways, when the driver and his passengers really saw America, and not just the exit to it.

Next to the travel table sat the "sea shell table". Similar in make-up to the travel table, encased under the glass were sea shells of all kinds. In the center was a perfect, white sand dollar. Radiating to the four corners were arms made of spiral conical shells, gradually increasing from thumbnail size to the length of my index finger at the corners. Scattered among the triangular spaces remaining were shells of all kinds; conk shells, mussel shells, more sand dollars, crab shells, sea urchin shells, starfish, and even the occasional seahorse. Collected from Florida to Southern California, and from the Great Lakes to the Gulf of Mexico, they represented thousands of miles of travel over almost half a century.

Grandpa was a scavenger of most any genre and of great resource. He might help a friend or neighbor clean out their attic, and help himself to the discarded remains of the day. He would walk newly plowed fields looking for flint arrowheads (and constructed an "arrowhead table" that resided in the living room). He frequented estate sales, arriving early to closely inspect the treasures and craftily plan his bidding strategy. He accumulated gifts from the many friends he made on his frequent travels. It may have been his businessman personality, but he made friends easily with his amiable nature and gift of conversation. Few told a story as well as Grandpa. In his later days when his poor eyesight prevented him from driving, he would take long walks around town, and was not above sampling the more unique articles from the local trashcans.

Starting on the east side of the shelves, I looked at the familiar stacks of cigar boxes. Grandpa loved a good cigar, and that was always a safe birthday or Christmas gift for him. In retrospect it may not have been the cigars he loved, but it was the boxes. The boxes were the perfect storage container for most any artifact. Each was neatly labeled on the end of the box indicating the contents: shells, arrowheads, fossils, geodes, quartz. Out in his garage, a similar number of boxes were labeled nuts, bolts, nails, and screws.

Further down from the cigar boxes stood rows of glasses and bottles. Medicine bottles from the turn of the 20th century shared space with containers of more contemporary products such as Coca-Cola, Tab, and 7-Up. An eclectic display of Jim Beam whiskey bottles adorned a shelf, shaped as people, animals, cars, and imitation classical urns. There were glasses commemorating the Apollo Moon Landing, several runnings of the Kentucky Derby, and the comic *B.C.* As I had countless times before, I picked up a glass, noting the perfect circle absent of dust on the shelf that was left. After admiring the profile of the 1958 Derby winner TimTam, I carefully returned it to its clean resting place.

Next came the books and the magazines. His collection of old books was truly eclectic. I picked up a copy chronicling the sinking of the Titanic. Its cover was ripped and its spine suffered from compound fractures, but I had always been intrigued by the book. Printed in 1912, it was one of the first contemporary accounts of the incident. A home health primer from the early 1900's warned that blindness and impotence were potential side effects from masturbation. Other volumes of the library included textbooks on mathematics, German, and a history of Indiana, identifying it as a "progressive commonwealth."

The weight of a stack of *National Geographic* magazines bowed one of the shelves. The collection contained no issues with pictures on the cover, instead depicting only the magazines contents on a white background, trimmed in the familiar yellow border.

The final series of shelves contained the collection of articles difficult to categorize. A large brass bowl used for mixing chocolate and a candy scale were remnants of products made and sold at the bakery years ago. A collection of wooden-handled lathe tools were from his father, a former cabinet maker. He took up the trade of woodworking in retirement, making beautiful turned bowls and candlesticks, which he sold from his display shelves in the first floor bedroom. An old school slate, a small wooden whiskey cask with a brass spigot, and a large paper hornet's nest were all of unknown origins and significance, but were nonetheless articles that had long been on permanent display.

The diverse displays continued with no end: brass weights and scales in a wooden box, ceramic pickle crocs, copper wash tub, and two painted metal patio chairs so sturdy they may have been crafted from the discarded front fenders from a Hudson Hornet. A "girlie" calendar from the 1960's adorned the west wall. Seated provocatively on a pool table, she wore only a skimpy two-piece bikini painted on a clear plastic sheet that covered the picture. Upon lifting the plastic cover, her true assets were revealed.

As I surveyed the collection, I thought about all the times this museum served as a refuge from all the "adult talk". I could lose myself in imagining what "Andy Womak's Motor Hotel" of Flagstaff, Arizona looked like. I could be transported to beaches all across the country, or to the canyons of the great Southwest. I could even travel back in time, among the early inhabitants of North America, or the bizarre animals and plants of an unknown pre-historic era. In Grandpa's museum, anything was possible with a fertile imagination.

I turned back to look at the empty stairwell. I imagined his large frame slowly descending the stairs. His features turned from shadow to flesh once he was at the bottom of the stairs and in the light bulb's glow. The light reflected in his glasses, his forehead prominent with thin gray and brown hair combed straight back to the crown of his head. I might ask him to identify some relic, or where he collected certain artifacts. Usually some interesting story ensued, and was interrupted by my Mom or Dad saying it was time to go.

But today the curator would not make an appearance. Today's tour was self-guided before the museum closed forever. I pulled the dirty white cord and watched as the glowing filament went black. Grabbing the pipe on my left, I slowly exited the exhibit area for the last time.

Some of Grandpa's collection was retained and treasured by the family, and some was sold in the estate sale. Sadly, most was piled in the trash to be forgotten forever…or, as I like to believe, perhaps to be rescued by some other collector on an early morning perambulation.

A Baker's Life

Bakery crew of the Diekman Bake-Rite Bakery, New Castle, Indiana, circa 1925. George and Carl Diekman are first from the left, respectively.

Notice to the Reader: It is recommended that, to obtain the best appreciation for this and the following story, the reader mentally provide their best gravelly, 90 year old "Hoosier drawl" for the narrative.

"All my grandparents came from Germany. Likely they worked in the furniture factories and did some farmin'. My grandfather, Fredrick Dickman, was uh homeopathic doctor. He would drive uh horse 'n buggy to people's homes to treat'em, often being paid in barter."

Fredrick H. Dickman, Johanna Frederika Lorenz, Jacob Klund, and Catherine Eberhardt were all part of the flood of European migration that washed over the United States in the mid-1800s. All were seeking opportunities for a better life in the new country of the United States; opportunities that were hard to find in war-torn and economically depressed central Europe. Fredrick Dickman arrived in Baltimore, Maryland in the fall of 1845, and worked his way west as a shoemaker and shopkeeper until settling around Shelbyville, Indiana in 1858. Not long after his arrival, his first wife Catherine died, leaving him alone to raise six small children in a new home. Four months later, he married Johanna Lorenz, who had only been in America for two years. The shoemaker and storekeeper studied and practiced homeopathic medicine, gave "some attention" to farming, and had interest in a woolen mill. He and Johanna had seven children of their own; their youngest son born May 6, 1874, they named George Conrad.

Following his compulsory military service, Jacob Klund, along with his brother John and his sister Margaret, left Mulhofohen, Germany in 1869 for Brooklyn, New York. A year later he heeded the call west, and settled to farming and furniture factory work in Shelbyville, Indiana. With his new bride Catherine Eberhardt, who recently arrived to America from Bellingheim, Germany, they had seven children, with four surviving into adulthood. The youngest daughter they named for her mother; Catherine Eberhardt Klund.

"We all lived about uh mile an uh half north of the cemetery on the Knightstown Road there in Shelbyville. My father and Uncle Wally Weakley worked in the furniture factories, even though they lived on the farm. In the wintertime they worked in the factory, cause in the summer you raised the crops."

The boy that would become the baker was born on that farm on the Knightstown Road May 25, 1902. He was the second child of George C. and Catherine E. Diekman; his sister Marie Anna, was six years his senior.

"Its uh mystery how Dickman became Diekman. All we know is my dad said it was Diekman, not Dickman. Course that's not right, cause it says D-I-C-K-M-A-N right on Grandpa's grave. It could be Dad got tired of be'in kidded in school about "Dick"man. My cousin Margaret Weakley, she married Floyd Carr, and every time we'd have uh big get together, Floyd would kid me that my dad was a horse thief, that's why he changed it to D-I-E-K-M-A-N."

"About six families lived in uh mile an' uh quarter radius, and we'd get together all the time and played dominos, pulled taffy, and had popcorn. I liked for Dad to carry me home, but he never would. They would all butcher together. There was uh man by the name of Lewis had equipment, and they would all butcher together in uh barn lot. My dad had worked for uh time in uh butcher shop in Columbus, Indiana before I was born. They would make sausage an' cure hams an' all; it was uh big time."

"Grandma Klund lived on Taylor Street in Shelbyville, and she was uh wun'erful cook. She could only eat wild meat, an' she cooked in uh big iron pot till the meat fell off the bones. She would never eat at the table with us; always sat at a little table by the stove. She often just had broth, cause she had uh sour stomach. She would like to sit in her rocker, and she would have hard candy in her pocket. The grandchildren would stand quietly next to her as she rocked, and she would give us candy every now an' again."

In 1908 George Diekman and his brother-in-law Wally Weakley bought a bakery at 921 Broad Street in New Castle. George, Catherine, Marie, and six year old Carl loaded their worldly possessions in a wagon, hooked up the team of horses, and traveled the sixty miles to their new home, above the bakery in "the flats" of New Castle.

"I was raised in uh bakery. I would come home from school and wrap bread. Dad put an apron on me, and I would do things to help out. I wouldn't do much ya' know, but I was learnin'."

George later moved the retail part of the bakery to the center of town on Broad Street, across the street from the county courthouse. It initially shared store space with a butcher shop; the glass case of breads, cakes and cookies stood opposite sides of butchered beef hanging from giant hooks anchored in the ceiling, dripping blood onto beds of sawdust on the floor.

The family moved to a house at 17th and Indiana Avenue, and Marie and Carl enjoyed playing ball games on the dirt covered Broad Street on the east end of town. "We would do like all kids did; throwin' rocks, runnin' around and hidin'. We'd play games like 'Go Sheepy Go' and 'Duck on Davey'. The carnival or circus would come to town, an' Dad would give us fifty cents to go see it."

In fact once when the carnival came to town, Marie had her first date, and asked her father for permission to go. He gave her permission only if she agreed to take her little brother along. She never asked his permission again, even to marry.

George Diekman was a stocky man with large hands and a broad face that frequently contained an equally broad smile. "He was uh pretty strong willed man who could do anything he set his mind to. He was uh man of good common sense, an' he had uh lot of friends. He kept the family together. Dr. Fredrick Dickman had two families, and we was always close with all the ones, aunts and uncles, with the second family. We'd get together uhbout ev'ry month up until Dad died, an' that was the last of the get togethers."

"Dad had uh temper. Once at the dinner table he told me to get up and wash my hands better. When I got into the kitchen, I thumbed my nose at him.

There was uh mirror in the dining room buffet, an' he could see me in the mirror out in the kitchen thumbing my nose and I got a good whippin'.'"

George, like many laborers of that period, wore many hats. In addition to the bakery, he worked at the Jesse French Piano Factory, and worked a farm with an orchard, hogs, and pigs. "Well, back then ya' know, if you weren't gifted, ya' had uh hard time gettin' by. Ya' had to be able to do differ'nt things. They rented uh farm, and worked in the factory. They repaired their own shoes. My dad would go huntin' rabbits with uh neighbor, Mr. Murl, who had ferrets. Ya' put a ferret down a rabbit hole and they put uh sack over the hole. I can remember them comin' home with 25, 30 rabbits each. They would skin'em, and I remember Dad hangin' them up on the clothesline and lettin'em freeze."

"Mom was shorter than Dad; wasn't uh big women. She had uhlot of patience. I can't remember her losin' her temper. She was uh damn good cook and baker. Every weekend she would make kuchen, which was like uh coffee cake. She'd take bread dough, poke holes in it, and put brown sugar and butter in the holes. I would always try to get the piece with the most holes in it, cause that's where most of the butter an' brown sugar was."

"Dad wasn't hard to work for. In fact, I was just uh kid and I think I was harder on him than he was on me. He give me hell once in uh while. I remember one time he chased me 'round the bench, but he never caught me. He wasn't too hard on me. He didn't give me any more than I deserved."

Diekman's Bake-Rite Shop at 1222 Broad Street had two expansive storefront windows filled with displays of wrapped bread, rolls, cakes, and doughnuts. Signs reading 'Old Fashion Salt Rising Bread' were featured prominently in each window. A tent awning shaded the storefront; its scalloped front edge boldly reading 'Bake-Rite Bakery'.

Upon entering a long two-tiered display case ran along the left side of the store. Frosted cakes sat in the lower display case, while pies, doughnuts, and cookies filled the two shelves of the upper display case. Two large bell jars of cookies sat like sentries at the end of the top case. Taller cases with sliding glass doors were against the wall behind the main display case, with wrapped bread neatly stacked on the shelves.

The shop was truly a family enterprise. Customers might find George, Katie, Marie, or Carl serving them behind the case. Marie's youngest son LeRoy swept the floor before school, wanting to be sure to finish before his grandfather arrived because 'Grandpa had a particular way a floor had to be swept, and if you didn't do it that way, you did it again!'

The bakeshop had at its heart a huge workbench for working out the dough. Piles of dough sat on the well-floured surface of the table. Scattered amongst the dough were solid wood rolling pins as thick as a man's leg, massive shallow bowels for carrying flour, and a dough encrusted dual platform balance scale. Scattered all around were cooling racks, barrels of flour and sugar, and cans of lard. Two revolving ovens, one electric and one gas, sat along one wall in the back.

"The gas oven was always on. We rarely used the electric oven cause there was too many outages at the light plant. When the electricity went off you'd have to hand crank the revolving oven to keep from burnin' the bread or cakes or whatever you had in there at the time."

In the fall of 1919, at the age of 17, Carl first succumbed to the wanderlust that would be a regular part of his life. "I was uh sophomore in high school, and I decided I wanted to go to California. Mom or Dad never said I could or couldn't go, so I left school an' went. Mother and my sister Marie fixed me a shoebox full of sandwiches and took me to the train station. I took the Pennsylvania train to Chicago, an' took an omnibus from the Pennsylvania station to the Santa Fe station."

"While a'waitin' for the train at the Santa Fe station, I saw a group of workin' cowboys...I don't mean dude cowboys...workin' cowboys with their old sweaty black hats, chaps, and empty holsters (cause they left their guns wherever they was a'stayin'). They had brought a load of cattle to the stockyards. For a kid of 17 years old to see about 20 real cowboys, that was quite a treat."

"In New Mexico I saw my first real Indians. When I was in New Mexico an' on intuh Arizona I remember lookin' out of the window and seein' thousands of white skeletons layin' out on the side of the railroad tracks. At first I thought they was cattle, but I found out later they was buffalo. They hired hunters to ride the trains to kill the buffalo. Left the carcasses right where they were at for the wolves and the buzzards. Went back out to California in 1945 and thought I'd see'um, but there wasn't a one of them skeletons. They probably picked them up and grounded them up for chicken feed, cause bone meal makes the egg shells harder."

"Dad had wrote his friend Mel Rynearson in Long Beach to look for me uh job. I worked in uh bakery on Pine Street, making cakes. I got pretty fast at icin' cakes. I got to where I could ice 100 layer cakes in an hour. I came home in March 1920; I guess I got uh little home sick."

Two months later, a chance meeting on a rainy day would change his life forever. "It was Memorial Day, and Reese Miller and I was goin' to the Speedway. We stopped intuh Mitch's Drug Store on the corner of 18th and C Avenue. He had uh soda fountain, and we stopped to get uh Coke. There was uh girl a'sittin' at uh table. Mr. Mitch comes over to us and says, 'Say, you boys got uh umbrella, why don't you take this girl home.' We went outside, and I says to Reese Miller (it was his umbrella), I says, 'Reese, you go on home and I'll take this girl home', which she lived out at the corner of 25th and Walnut. That was the meetin' of my wife. That was 1920, Memorial Day, and we was married December 4, 1920."

"Her father had uh little grocery store and she worked the grocery store and I delivered bread to the grocery store so I got to see her every once an' awhile. We dated about once uh week to start with, then it got to be about every day. When we had uh family get together at Shelbyville, I'd invite her along with Father, Mother and I when we would go to the 'big feeds' over tuh Shelbyville."

"I don't remember proposin' to her other than sayin' 'let's go to Kintucky and get married' (Marie was only 15, and she couldn't get married in Indiana). We got on the train at the Pennsylvania station, and it was rainin'. Her sisters Marian and Martha went to the station with us to see us off. We went down to Cincinnatuh; then the railroad station was right downtown on the south east end of town, right on the river. We went to the Grand Hotel on Fountain Square. We got a room there, and then we got uh taxi cab to take us over to Newport to get married."

"That was a Saturday, and he took us to the courthouse, and the courthouse was closed. He said, 'I'm not sure you can get married today'. I was afraid for a minute I'd have tuh put a note on our hotel room door 'License Applied For', cause ya' know then when ya' bought a car you never got your license right away, so you put that sign on your car. I was afraid I was going to have to put that on our bedroom door…to make it legal ya' know!"

"But that cabbie, he knew all the ropes ya' know; he had taken lots of other couples tuh get married. So he round up the Justice of the Peace, and we got married. There was an oyster house about uh block from the Grand Hotel, and that's where we ate. They shucked the oysters right there, so you know'd they were fresh."

"After we got married we lived with my folks, and that's when Marie learned how to cook. She didn't know anything about cooking at all. But once she got started, she loved to cook and she turned out to be uh pretty good cook herself."

Carl and Marie were a married couple for only ten months and ten days, when they became a family with the birth of a son, Carl Junior Diekman, who they affectionately called Bud. "Bud's real name is Carl Junior Diekman, not Carl Diekman, Jr. Marie did that; I didn't have anything to do with that."

The new family rented a five-room house on Grand Avenue, which Carl was able to completely furnish (except for a stove) with his life savings of $350. "My Dad started me to savin' money when I was uh kid. He'd give me uh quarter every week, and I'd save up till I'd have uh dollar, and then I'd put that in the bank."

In addition to his talent of saving money, his talent for making money as a businessman was beginning to show. "In the winter of 1921 Father and Mother went to Hollywood, Florida, and left me to run the bakery. Well, there was uh flour salesman by the name of Ed Stone from Carthage, Missourah. I bought a carload of flour off him, and he says 'Carl', he says, 'if you buy another second carload of flour, I'll guarantee ya' uh dollar uh barrel on that by the time you get it in the bakery.' Then a barrel of flour was two bags, 98 pounds each bag and the cost was $5.00 uh barrel. By the time I got the other carload of flour in, it had gone up uh dollar uh barrel, so I had got that much profit for my Father. Of course I never got any of it, but I got the glory knowin' I'd made that much profit just off of flour."

George and his son Carl made the Diekman Bake-Rite Bakery profitable. "There was five bakeries in New Castle, and one other wholesale bakery on 18th and I Avenue; twice the size of my Father's. But we had our share of the business." Carl moved his family into a house on 9th Street and on March 13, 1927, to the surprise of almost everyone, the family grew to four with the birth of a daughter, Lou Anna.

"There wasn't uh soul knew Marie was pregnant; not the bakers, not the grocer, not our friends we played cards with. But we went with Mom and Dad to uh carnival over tuh Chesterfield, and uh female fortune-teller told Marie she was pregnant, and that her child had no future. Well, after that it was on Marie's mind all the time. She told Dr. Stout, and he said everything would be fine."

"Dr. Stout and Marie delivered in the dining room of the house on 9th Street. Marie asked if the baby was alright, and he said, 'yes, it's a perfect girl'. Marie relaxed and just shook all over, but she got settled down after uh while, and everything was alright."

"Dad sold the bakery on contract, and we all moved to Florida in 1928 with the intent of buying uh bakery, which I could have bought but there was no summer business. The big hotels boarded their places up in the summertime. We rented a house in Hollywood for $25, furnished." One year-old Lou Anna, just recently walking, would repeatedly try to follow her older brother across a vacant lot as he walked to school. Each time her trek would be abruptly halted by painful sand spurs in her bare feet, and she was left standing in the lot crying until her Grandpa Diekman came to the rescue. Carl and George worked at a bakery in Hollywood, and supplemented their income by making souvenir crafts for sale: pine needle baskets and shell encrusted pottery.

The slower paced southern lifestyle they enjoyed was suddenly changed by 'The Hurricane'. "It was centered in Palm Beach and went over to Okahchobee; hunerd 'n five mile per hour winds at Hollywood. It blew big ships out of the bay and right up next tuh the big hotels. It took all the water out of the west end of Lake Okahchobee, and it was 20 feet deep! Last account from the Miamuh Hearald was there was 3,500 people lost their lives, but the actual count of the bodies found and buried was 2,200 and some. A lot of the bodies were blown out in the everglades."

"I worked in the bakery there in Hollywood till we used up all the flour, cause the water was an inch deep on the floor, and we had to mix up all the bread dough by hand. So he closed the bakery and we moved to Fort Lauderdale and got a job there cause the bakery helper was called up to the National Guard to go out to Lake Okahchobee and bury all the dead. I had made up my mind we was going back to New Castle."

"Uncle Wally wrote and told me about a retail bakery in Rushville. As soon as I got back, I went down to look at it, then talked to Dad about it and he thought it was uh good buy. Well, when we came back from Florida I didn't have any money saved, so I rented the 9th Street house, and we lived with

Marie's folks until I was able to trade my equity in the 9ᵗʰ Street house for the building on 2ⁿᵈ Street in Rushville that would become the Quality Bake Shop. That was March 9ᵗʰ, 1929, so we lived here in Rushville since then, and I owned and operated the Quality Bake Shop for 35 years."

Carl converted the two-story store into a bakery. The location close to the railroad tracks would make it convenient for unloading the boxcar loads of flour. "A little store like ours, you'd never think you'd buy uh carload of flour, but we did. We sold uh lot of bread."

The family moved to a two-story house on Buena Vista Street, also adjacent to the railroad tracks. Lou Anna could recall sitting out on the roof watching as President Herbert Hoover gave a whistle stop campaign speech from the back of his decorated Pullman car. Lou Anna would also recall less famous visitors, who rode in the boxcars, and would knock on their back door looking for something to eat, and Marie made sure they never went away hungry. Starting a new small business as the country fell into the economic abyss of the Great Depression would have seemed either very unlucky timing or sheer folly, yet Carl made his new business a success.

"There was uh lot of people out of work, but we had an item everybody had to have; bread. We had to work hard. We worked hard, long hours. But I can truthfully say I made money all during the Depression. I sold yeast bread for uh nickel uh loaf, but I never sold salt risin' bread for less than ten cents uh pound loaf. Now, it didn't cost but a very, very little more for uh pound of salt risin' than uh pound of yeast bread, but there wasn't everybody that could make salt risin' bread and so I never did sell it less than ten cents uh loaf".

They worked hard long hours indeed. Carl would start his typical workday at 2:00am, unless it was a Friday or Saturday, when the workday might actually start the night before. The first order of business for he and his baker's helper would be to prepare all the dough. "Once we got all the dough made, then we would make the fried rolls to go out to the restaurants by 5:00am, and I'd carry the rolls out to the restaurants on uh tray with uh cloth over the top.

We'd make cake donuts and yeast donuts, and then the bun dough and roll dough would be ready, and then last would be the bread dough; the yeast and the salt risin'. "

"Course the salt risin' was the big item that we made. The salt risin' formula came with the business. A man, George Wilkinson, and his wife started makin' salt risin' bread in their home and delivered it in baskets to around the homes in Rushville. Back then they had the old time recipe, and the housewife had to take the starter to bed with them, cause if the starter ever got cold it was no good. Course later Coleman at New York developed a salt risin' meal; that way it wasn't so hard to make."

"On our smallest day we'd make 100 loaves, and on Friday and Saturday we'd make between 800 an' uh thousand loaves. Friday bread would go to Connersville; Slickte's Grocery Store in Connersville, they sold uh lot. A.B. Woods down at Greensburg got 120 loaves. Now Tompkins at Milroy never got theirs till Saturday mornin'. They got 100 loaves every Saturday mornin' and they'd have it sold before the bread come up. Everybody would order their bread before."

"Three times uh week I'd take bread up to City Market in Indianapolis; salt risin' bread, gluten bread, and gluten cookies. On the way I'd stop to deliver at Carthage, Knightstown, and Greenfield. Then on the way home the first stop would be at this tavern across from the factory. They always had good tenderloin sandwiches, so I'd have me uh tenderloin sandwich and uh draft beer, and then head home."

Carl's bakery was located at 128 W. 2nd Street in Rushville. It had a shiny white tiled store front, with a row of black tile along the bottom that reflected the shoes of the pedestrians as the hustled along the busy street. A large display window dominated the storefront, displaying the bountiful baked goods. Above the door on the right side of the storefront in black tile art deco lettering was the name "Quality Bake Shop". Just like the bakery he was raised in, Carl's bakery was a family operation. Marie worked in the front of the store with a store girl, with Lou Anna helping. " Just like my dad did me, I put an apron on Bud and had him help in the bakery. Marie didn't like me puttin' an apron on Bud, but he didn't do much…it was uh learning experience". Lou Anna was artistically inclined, and as she got older, she frequently decorated the large display windows in front. During World War II, posters exhorting patrons to 'Send our Boy's Boxes', or encouraging the country to 'Get in the Scrap' (poised over a diarama of toy army men) graced the window. Once a year she made a 'Gone Fishin'' poster to hang in the window. Carl and Marie would close the shop for a week each year, get Marie's sister Marian to watch the kids, and hit the road on vacation. They frequently had no travel plan; just wherever the road and their inclinations took them.

Carl and the business became a fabric of the community. He cultivated business and social ties through his long time membership in the Eagles and Elks clubs. Though he was a life long supporter of the Democratic party (he was even asked to run for mayor once, but declined saying he could not take the time away from his business), he supported favorite son Republican candidate Wendell Willkie in the 1940 presidential election. He sent loaves of his famous salt rising bread to influential patrons and politicos emblazoned with the words 'Rise with Willkie'. He delivered bakery products daily to The Durbin Hotel, just a block away from his store, which served as Willkie's campaign headquarters. During the war Quality Bake Shop bread found its way to North Africa, Europe, and Asia as part of cherished 'boxes from home'. Carl became a partner in a tavern in town, but preferred his association be kept silent, because in his eyes, it wouldn't seem right for the proprietor of a family-oriented business.

Carl's business success was diametrically opposed to his father's business struggles. Unlike his son, George ultimately became a casualty of the Depression.

"Father wasn't doing too good in the bakery. He said, 'Used to be I could get money ahead, and now I can't get ahead'. He had to sell one farm, and had to

71

turn over the other farm and two lots in Florida to me. The farm at Millville was 240 acres of flat, level farm land, but in the Depression corn was three cent uh bushel and hogs were three dollars uh hun'erd. You just couldn't make any money on the farm. Somebody filed suit against him for payment on the farm, and it worried the life out him and he told me, 'I just don't know what to do'."

"He just lost his mind, stayin' awake all night. I went up there to try to talk to him. I told him to take a drink of whiskey to calm him down. He never drank, except for medicine, but he took a drink. Well that made him worse. Well, we was afraid that…well, you just don't know what a person does when they lose their mind ya' know. Maybe they might try to kill ya', cause he was uh strong willed man. He never got mad very often, but when he was mad, he was mad. Same as me. We was just afraid of Dad…didn't know what he was going to do, so we put him in jail. A policeman came, and once he was in jail he hollered the whole time. Attorney got him entered to the hospital over tuh Richmond. I followed the police car over tuh Richmond. I didn't want him tuh get upset."

"Something happened over there. I'm sure they gave him shock treatment. Then he had a cerebral hemorrhage over there and passed away."

"After Father passed away, Aunt Marie and Uncle Ed moved in with Mom, which was right in uh way, but in uh way not since it wasn't really her home then. She lived ten years after Father passed away. I took the bakery over, which was right since I had money in it, an' I ran both places until I was able to sell it. They was each buried over in Shelbyville, because that was their home."

Sunday, December 7th, 1941. "We was at 21st and Grand Avenue in New Castle when we heard about the bombin' of Pearl Harbor on the car radio." Bud joined the Marine Corps as soon as he graduated, and before he was due to report for basic training, Carl thought a trip with his son was in order.

"He and I drove straight through to Florida. When we got down there, we saw a flyer to go to Cuba; three days for $18, everything included. Well hell, ya' can't beat that. Marie and I had seen the boats leavin' for Cuba before; big white ships with people all dressed up a'wavin' goodbye. Well we had to be down at the docks at 7:00am, and when we got there, there was this little ol' dinky boat, painted green. We got on, and it didn't leave until 11:00 at night. During the war you see. We didn't know it but in the papers there was uh German U-boat that had sunk a ship right off the coast of Miamuh."

"The next mornin' we heard shots. We ran up on deck, and we was part of a convoy of big ships. Two airplanes was flyin' around the ships the whole time. We followed them a while till they turned to go off to the Panama Canal, and we went to Cuba."

"There was four on the tour; us and an ex-soldier and an ex-marine. We stayed in uh nice old hotel right in downtown Cuba. It was cheap, but the rooms was clean an' the food was good. A limousine driver come to take us to several night clubs. The ex-soldier and ex-marine told me they'd likely be drinkin' uh lot, an' asked me to keep their money an' pay all the bills. We went to several clubs, an' then these guys said they wanted to see the Cuban circus. Well we didn't know what that was, but they did. There was these women in there, and they did sex every way you know, then after they was through, they wanted to take us to uh room, but we left and went to another club. It was uh pretty nice club with uh lady that was uh good singer, and I danced with her. She came over to the table (she knew the limousine driver), and I danced with her, and she was very nice and decent. But that was quite an experience."

Bud had his basic training on the east coast, and ultimately shipped out from San Diego, serving on Iwo Jima. "You're worried, but you take it in stride. Bud was lucky that he wasn't maimed or killed, but when he came back he was uh broken man 'cause he was taught to take orders and not give orders. He got back in the bakery, and he was uh good baker but he couldn't give orders telling others what to do. Had he been uh person who could manage he would still be in business today here in Rushville 'cause that was uh goin' business, but he couldn't make it go."

After a brief retirement, Carl came back to the bakery in order to get it on solid financial footing so it could be sold. Bud moved his family to California, and provided the perfect destination for the retired wanderers; now free to pursue the road whenever it called.

"We had uh lot of happy times together. All the trips we took together. We enjoyed life to the fullest you might say. Marie loved traveling just as much as I did. We never had any fixed place to go. If we wanted to stop some place for uh day or two we'd stop. If we wanted to keep uh-goin', we'd keep uh-goin'. We'd been a lot of nice places and seen uh lot, and enjoyed life to the fullest."

MAKIN' THE SALT RISIN'

Storefront of the Diekman Bake-Rite Bakery, New Castle, Indiana, circa 1925. This is where Carl Diekman learned his craft.

The Reverend James Schaffer's wavy hair was about the same color as his white vestments. Standing at the podium next to the head of the casket, he pulled a few folded pages from his pocket at the same time he was putting on his glasses, and began the eulogy for my grandfather. I knew the story well. Carl G. Diekman, born May 25th, 1902 outside of Shelbyville, Indiana. Devoted husband to Margaret Marie for 68 years, 22 days. Father to Carl Junior and Lou Anna. Grandfather to eight, Great-Grandfather to eleven, and Great-Great-Grandfather to one. In addition to being a long time member, at one time or another, of most any community organization with an animal mascot, he was a neighbor and friend of the Rushville, Indiana community for 66 years.

"A master baker", Reverend Schaffer said, "providing the community the tasty products of his hands. Hours of kneading the dough to make his specialty salt-rising bread." If there was one thing I knew well, it was the local fame of the "Quality Bake Shop Salt Rising Bread". It had been used unsuccessfully in the 1940 presidential campaign against FDR, though I think even Wendell Willkie would agree it wasn't the bread's fault. It had played its part in defeating the Nazis and the Japanese in World War II, bringing a bit of home to the bellies of the boys at the front. It was even still being talked about in loving and longing tones by people paying their last respects, over 30 years after he had taken the last one-pound loaf out of the oven.

"Makin' the salt risin' " as he would say in his Hoosier drawl, had indeed made quite an impact, not just in his hometown, but also around the world. Such craft, whose product was lost almost as soon as it was created, deserves to be recorded for history. No one better to provide the honors than the master baker himself.

"You'd buy the white corn meal with the culture in it. All we'd hafta do is twelve hours before we'd set the yeast, we'd scald powdered milk and the corn meal with the culture in it and let it set twelve hours. When we would come tuh work in the mornin', why that'id be the first thing we'd do is stir that yeast. Then we'd let that set uh half hour, then we'd make a sponge. Then that sponge would have to sit for uh couple of hours. Within a couple of hours it would rise up to the top of the bowl, and then it would start to goin' down. Just as it started to goin' down in the center, we would take it right at that time, and stir it up, and if you'd take uh deep breath while you was doin' that, why it would knock you out; the fumes would come up there, and just like drinkin' a big glass of whiskey, you'd get drunk right away. Then we'd stir that down, divide it, and put it into another bowl. Then we'd pour hot water in there, not warm but hot water, and start a' mixin' in sugar and salt, and when we got enough flour in there, we poured in the hot lard last."

"When we were makin' uh full batch, that was 420 one pound loaves, so it took two Hobart 80 quart mixers to mix it. As soon as it was mixed up just enough so no lard was loose, we'd throw that out on the bench. And I was the one that scaled that off in one pound two ounce loaves. I got so I could scale it pretty darn fast. I'd put it in the bolder and it would come out the other end formed in a loaf of bread. Course there was flour on the belt there. If the man on the other end wasn't fast enough, why he'd get stacked up and I'd hafta rest a minute till he got caught up. But Carlus Heath was pretty fast, and he'd swipe the loafs with a brush with hot lard on it, and fill up uh rack. We'd get uh rack full, that's 420 loaves, run that in the proof box and let that proof up, and then put it in the oven. At first we had the hearth oven. We'd put the bread on the peel (that's a wooden paddle ya' know, about eight inches wide and thirty inches long, with uh long handle on it), and I got so I could push that back and just slip the peel out and the pan would slide right in the corner. I'd just keep loading it up. I had a double deck oven and got it loaded up."

"When it got time to take the bread out, I was generally the one to take the bread out of the oven. I'd dump it out on the rack, and then either Carlus Heath, or Raymond Kiskee who worked for me, or Louie Salger would take the bread off there with cloth mits and put it on the rack. Pretty hot job, but then, ya' get so ya' get used to it. All the bread then had to be wrapped with a wrapper. We just had a one-loaf wrapper. Use sheets about so big (the baker using his hands to demarcate a square about shoulder width), lay a loaf of bread on there, fold that over, and put that on the wrapper and that'd come down and fold the ends up, and push it through and there's a hot plate there that sealed it shut, and you put another loaf in and that loaf would push the other loaf off the hot plate. Once you got about half uh dozen loaves wrapped, the ones that was coming off was cool enough, and they would drop into uh box or basket. Then you'd take'm off of there and put'em on uh rack or take'm into the store."

A few years before he died, he commented that he had tried to make salt rising bread once again at home, put he was never quite successful. Perhaps it was the lack of the ingredients bought in barrel and trainload quantities. Maybe it was not having the power of an 80-quart Hobart mixer, or the fire of a big double deck hearth oven. Whatever the reason, we can be sure it had nothing to do with the master baker's hands. Though wrinkled and bent from his 90 years, they were still nimble and quick, ever guided by love.

Part Two:
Histories Present

The Robert Van Zant family, Mother's Day at the Durbin Hotel,
Rushville, Indiana, 1962. Decked out in their Sunday best are, left to right,
Robert, Scott, Rex, and Lou Anna

THE SECRET OF SURVIVAL
OF LITTLE BROTHERS

A scene of sibling serenity, Nogales, Mexico, 1965.
Rex is on the left, and I am on the burro.

Sibling rivalry has long been a serious issue; just ask Abel. The eldest child of every family at some point in time has asked themselves, "Why did my parents have this child?" Such a decision must certainly defy logic in their minds. After all, if they have already given birth to the best, why mess with a good thing? Another child only means having to share time and resources while having to endure loud cries and foul smelling diapers. To the oldest child, it's a no win situation.

I'm sure that must have been my older brother's perspective when I arrived. He was five years old and already had adjusted to a sister two years his junior who was a special needs child. The advent of another baby imposed upon his last full year of youthful leisure before he began school was probably more than he could bear.

Little brothers identify in big brothers a larger version of themselves. Unlike adults, who seem almost like a different species, older brothers are young enough to be identified as kids but larger and wiser with abundantly more life experience (relatively speaking). They are examples to emulate and roles in which to aspire.

Big brothers identify little brothers as an inferior version of themselves. These little brothers are smaller and weaker, run slower, can't tie their own shoes, need to take naps, and wet the bed. Worst of all, they always want to tag along and are always getting in the way. In short, they severely cramp your style.

All things considered, it is a wonder that younger brothers live into maturity. A prime example of this principle occurred when I was about eight years old. Mom had asked my brother to take the trash out to the trash barrel in the back yard. Much to his chagrin I'm sure, I naturally followed him along on his errand. After dumping the trash in the barrel and returning toward the house, my brother threw the small steel wastebasket over the fence, placed his two hands at shoulder level on top of the wood frame for the metal wire fence, and kicked his right leg out and up to the side. After its push from the ground, his left leg followed in kind. I watched in awe as he turned ninety degrees in the air and gracefully "stuck the landing" in the tall grass on the other side of the fence. Without hesitation I ran up to the tall fence, and reached well above my head to the top. I gave a violent kick up and out with my right leg, while struggling to pull myself up with both arms. To my delight (and a bit of surprise), I found myself (or at least my trunk and right leg) resting on top of the fence. I went to push off the top of the fence and gauged my landing to approximate both the form and distance of my brother. Unfortunately I neglected to consider my tardy left leg, and caught my left foot on the top of the fence. I also "stuck the landing"; stuck it right on my face, with my forehead catching the sharp metal edge of the trashcan still lying on the ground.

Once he heard my shriek, my brother turned to find me rolling on the ground, my small hands covering my face, blood streaming between my fingers. Through the din of my pitiful cries, I heard my brother holler toward the house, "Mom, Scott hurt himself again," quickly adding, "and I didn't touch him!"

Ours was one of the first small ranch homes that grew out of an old Indiana cornfield like the dandelions that sprouted in our yard each spring. Behind us there were always two or three new home construction sites that attracted the area kids like ants to a picnic. The state of partial construction was eerily similar to the state of deconstruction we saw weekly on television series like *Combat!*, or re-runs of World War II era movies. We all gathered our toy armaments, broke up into squads, and repeatedly took the same French farmhouse, alternating roles as either the Allied Armed Forces or the Wehrmacht.

Occasionally, when the thrill of the self generated sounds of weapons (we got so good we could impersonate both Allied and German weapons) wasn't enough, and when the troop sizes were large enough, our imaginary projectiles gave way to more tangible ones. Construction sites always had plenty of piles of dirt, and the dried earth created abundant dirt clods of various sizes. We would divide the assembled mob into two armies of approximately equal size and strength. The oldest of each group was by default the general, and in the space of time it took for each soldier to collect all the ammunition he could carry, he developed a battle plan. We would gather together like football players in a huddle, as the general (usually my brother) drew out an intricate battle plan on the dusty ground using a handy crooked stick that would second as his riding crop (it seemed like all the fashionable generals on TV had riding crops). Invariably, the youngest and smallest of the troops (usually a small contingent of which I was always a member) took the advance position closest to the enemy. The general was quick to explain that my placement was logical because with my weak arm I couldn't throw as far, and so I had to be closer. "Besides," he would say, "you're smaller and harder to hit." While I couldn't argue with the general's logic, it did little to sway my fears of serving as cannon fodder for the impending dirt clod barrage.

During times of peace, the home construction sites served as perfect venues for bicycle stunt riding. Boards placed on bricks provided precision riding courses. Wide boards and bricks could also be used to construct ramps for jumping. These were the days of watching riders like Evil Knievel jumping over rows of cars parked side by side in some Las Vegas casino's parking lot. We all figured, "Hey, he had to start somewhere, right?"

After much discussion and eyeball engineering, our ramp took shape. We placed a couple of cement blocks between the two ramps representing a conservative distance to begin the competition. As we each succeeded at this distance, another block was added between the ramps thereby increasing the distance and continued in this fashion until passed or failed attempts ultimately led to our champion. While at the time I considered it a benevolent and gracious act, upon reflection I realize that my brother's insistence that I go first really meant I served as his bike jumping crash test dummy.

Growing up in the middle of the space race to the moon was an exciting time. Man's previous boundaries of vision, technology, and even the atmosphere no longer applied. Like every other kid of our generation, we wanted to be astronauts. We played with rocket and capsule space toys, read all the books and magazines about the space program, and watched every space launch on television. We were well aware of the rigorous training that every astronaut had to complete, and we wanted to do everything we could to prepare ourselves in advance.

We knew of the importance of simulator training in space flight, and so we developed our own flight simulator. We cleared out the center of our small bedroom closet, creating enough space between my parents hanging clothes for one of our chrome metal kitchen chairs. Once sitting on the yellow vinyl seat facing the open door, the astronaut would then be in position to read the control panel that had been painstakingly drawn on a cardboard box lid and taped to the back of the closet door. Once the astronaut was closed in the capsule (closet), his only means of seeing in the inky blackness of space was a regulation Boy Scout flashlight. (The closet light was only to be used in dire emergencies requiring the mission to be aborted.) The voice of mission control from beyond the door dictated the various situations of the flight simulation, and the subsequent reactions of the astronaut to the same.

For the maiden flight of our closet, I was chosen as the astronaut and my brother would serve as flight crew and mission control. With my astronaut helmet secured (which was actually a plastic toy German army helmet), I entered the closet and took my place on the kitchen chair. The ground crew secured me in the chair with a rope, made sure the control panel was in place, gave me the official Boy Scout flashlight, and secured the closet door. After the pre-flight check list was completed, we commenced the flight countdown; "10...9...8...7...6...5...4...ignition sequence start...3...2...1...ignition, we have ignition." Mission control followed my closet's progress down range, the nautical miles ever increasing until I achieved a stable orbit.

I think it was somewhere over Australia that I urgently hailed mission control for help. While attempting to execute a complicated pitch and yaw maneuver, the control panel fell off the door. "Houston, I have a serious equipment problem, over." I was answered with silence from the other side of the door. "Houston, I repeat I have an equipment problem, over." Again my plea was met with imaginary radio silence. A third and final attempt resulted in a similar response, and so I aborted the simulation mission, turned the closet light on, and opened the door. To my surprise, mission control was nowhere to be found. I found out later that mission control got bored and went out to ride his bike. Thankfully our simulator was not equipped with a closet door lock.

While luck may save a little brother from the occasional twisted logic or benign neglect heaped upon them by their big brothers, one can only explain through divine intervention how some actions of little brothers keep them from death's door. I can remember my brother being on vacation with our grandparents, and writing Mom at home, pleading with her to make sure "Scott keeps his grimy little hands off my stuff." Try as she might, Mom couldn't prevent me from doubling the strength of my GI Joe army by drafting my brother's doll, or enhancing my squadron strength by a model airplane or two. Invariably, as in all war, losses are incurred in battle. Broken rifles, landing gears, and propeller blades were common, and all incurred my brother's wrath.

Once when I was in middle school and my brother was in high school, we had the same band instructor. One day I happened to accidentally-on-purpose let slip my brother's unflattering impression of this teacher's personality. I think as a result my brother had to play the chromatic scale 500 times or something. My brother had to endure one year when we went to the same school (me in seventh grade, he a high school senior). I was a bit of a social wallflower, and so I would pass time at lunch doing odd things, like kicking a quarter against the up-sloping baseboards in the entry hallway. I enjoyed seeing how high up the wall the quarter would go. I came to find out that my brother did not find my recreation so appealing, as he implored our mom to "make him stop doing stupid, embarrassing things at school." I recall Mom having a little talk with me, but I'm sure if any behavior adjustments occurred, they were never probably enough in my brother's eyes to save him from complete social embarrassment.

The next year my brother went to college, and I'm sure to his great relief, was through with me on a regular basis. I eventually found my way in high school, largely due to the friends I made in sports. You see my brother was a sprinter on the track team, and he earned a letter jacket (though the school administrators made him cut his long hair before they would award it to him). I was sure I was going to be a sprinter too, but it didn't take long to see that I wasn't much of a sprinter, but I was a decent distance runner. I was able to follow in my brother's footsteps however; I earned a letter jacket too (as a sign of the changing social climate however, I was able to keep my long hair!)

I ultimately did survive to maturity as a little brother. And while I believe that a good degree of timely parental supervision and a little luck are key elements, I am convinced the **true** secret of survival of little brothers is the benevolence of big brothers.

THE BOYS OF SUMMER IN SUBURBIA

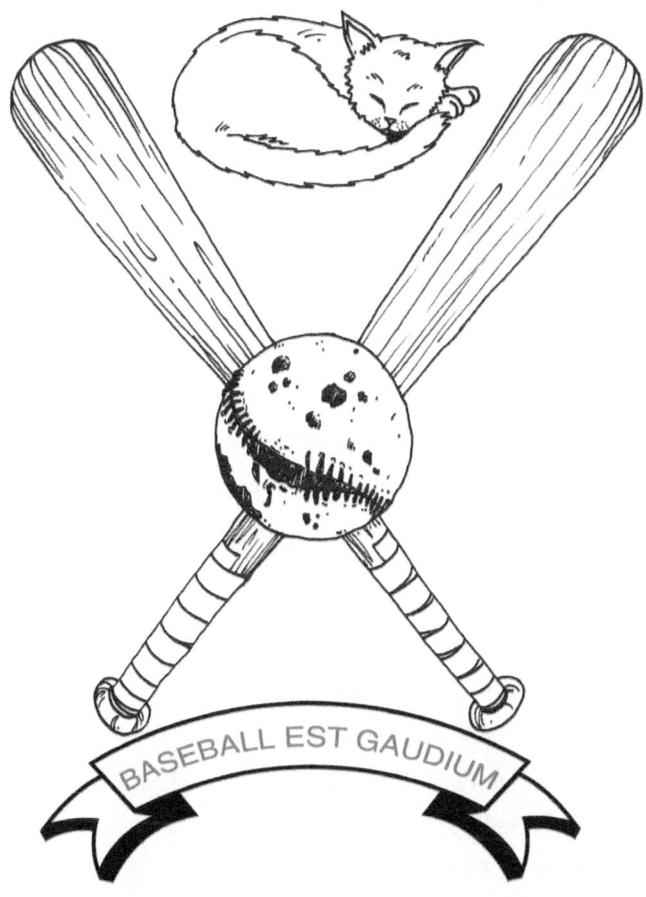

BASEBALL EST GAUDIUM

I thoughtlessly rolled the grass-stained ball in my right palm, the tips of my fingers nervously massaging the frayed red seams, as I stared intently at the scrap piece of wood about sixty feet in front of me that served as home plate. Silhouetted against the orange sky of the retreating sun, I could barely make out the face of Mike Abston as he stepped up to the plate. Tall and lanky, Mike exhibited unexpected power. With two outs and one man on, he represented the tying run. The order didn't get any easier after Mike, with Doug Newhouse and Mike Stokes to follow. All three were high school sophomores and packed plenty of pop in their bats. I knew I had to make my stand with Mike if we were to have any hopes of pulling off this upset.

Our young team of six kids, only two of which were even in high school, had been able to forge a lead over the passing innings. Though our opponents had "the big three" bashers in their line up, the remaining two elementary school kids in their line up presented at times glaring weaknesses both at bat and in the field. By constantly getting the expected outs and periodically retiring one of the big three in key situations (including me striking out Doug with the bases full of "ghost runners" to end the last inning) we were on the verge of taking the lead into the gloaming, when the appearance of fireflies usually signaled the end of the game. If I could get this out, the game would virtually be ours.

Words of encouragement poured in as my teammates positioned themselves behind me. Jim Stokes, Mike's younger brother, was both team captain and our left-handed left infielder, and he encouraged me to keep the ball down while he pounded his glove and got into his fielding crouch. Incorporating a modest shift for Mike, our right infielder John Matheny shuffled toward second base as he directed his younger brother Jack, our right fielder, to move toward right center. Randy Sorrell, whose father owned the vacant lot in which we played (and whom we honored by naming the ground "Sorrell Field"), went back to the row of tall weeds that marked the boundary of the next lot as well as the left field wall. The ground rules of Sorrell Field dictated that balls hit into the weeds in the air were an automatic out. While this rule was instituted as a practicality to limit the number of balls we lost, it certainly played to our distinct advantage this day as all three of the bashers were right handed. In center, Billy Edwards jogged deep to the Mulberry trees, where the weed wall and a white plank fence met. The white fence, badly in need of a paint job, marked the end of the neighboring trailer park while conveniently serving as our right field wall. Determined that nothing was going to go over his head, he was close enough to see the Arnold's cat resting on the sill of the front window of their house trailer just beyond the small cluster of trees. With the residential feeling provided by the trailer park in the background, we always had the feeling we were playing at Wrigley Field.

I kicked up a cloud of dirt with my blue US Keds, slapped the ball into my well-worn Leon Wagner model fielder's glove, gripped the ball with the seams, and started my windup. The shadow figure in front of me nervously twitched the bat in anticipation. I thought of all that had transpired in the summer to get to this point. The July 4th holiday was upon us, and the neighborhood baseball season was about to conclude. It all came to this moment. I strided forward with my left leg, and opened up my torso and shoulders to home as I pushed off with my right leg. Time seemed to slow down to a crawl as I felt the ball leave my fingertips, and I began to dream suburban summer thoughts.

Twenty years before, Sorrell Field and all the brick and wood-sided ranch houses that surrounded it was an Indiana cornfield. In the early fifties, it became a victim of urban sprawl. While it may be a bit of a stretch to call the sleepy city of New Castle "urban", the post-war housing explosion that resulted in ranch houses growing in fields outside of cities and towns happened even here. By 1969 the vacant fields were few and far between, lots merely biding their time until they too would host a modest home of their own. Sorrell Field, which gradually slanted down the left field line from its highest point at home, had the advantages of being regularly mowed, owned by someone whose kid liked baseball, and was contiguous with another open lot (thus minimizing the risk of window damage). Whenever we were able to raise enough kids to play a "serious" game, Sorrell Field was our home.

Serious games were however a rarity. The development of organized youth sport leagues were still years away, but between Little League, Pony League, and High School baseball, not many kids were available on a regular basis to play the semi-daily schedule of the "Suburban League". It was only the rare instance when the demands of organized league play, family vacation plans, and summer jobs left a window of opportunity for the serious suburban game. Usually around July 4th, just around All-Star Game time, we were able to get such a game together. This was our Suburban All-Star Game.

The real Suburban League of Western Road consisted of just three people: Jack Matheny, Tony Weintraut, and me. As the eldest (all of 11 years), I served as league commissioner, schedule coordinator, equipment supplier, and home field ground crew. The three of us would play short games in my "auxiliary" back yard. The rectangular open yard just beyond our fenced back yard was enclosed on the south by the back yard fence, the west by the neighbor's back yard fence, and on the north and east by regularly spaced peony bushes. A large maple tree rose from the center of the space, designating the pitcher's mound, and the area in direct line to the maple tree between two peony bushes on the east border served as home plate. The games were short for a number of reasons, not least of which was the relative attention spans of ten and eleven year olds. Tony always wanted to play his own team, even though among the three of us he was the weakest hitter. Even though we played pitcher's hand (if the pitcher gets the ball before the runner gets to first, the batter is out) and had several ground rules that worked to his advantage (fly balls over the fence and ground balls into the peony bushes along the right field line were all outs for Jack and I), we frequently made the ten-run mercy rule within the first three innings. Unlike the other kids our age who were interested in baseball, we didn't compete in the organized leagues. None of us were "gifted" with baseball talent, but in a cruel twist of fate, we loved the game. While these little games may not have done much to develop our playing skills, they did feed our desire for and love of the game.

On particularly warm days following our games, we would mount our single speed Schwinn bikes with their long "banana" seats and handle bars that resembled a Texas Longhorn steer, and ride down to A.B. Paul's Gulf filling station at the intersection of Western Road and busy State Highway 3. We would park our bikes next to the office, and line up in front of the tall Pepsi machine. We would drop in our quarter, open the skinny glass door on the left side of the machine, and pull out the desired bottled beverage by its neck. We popped open the cap using the built-in bottle opener, and quickly covered the top of the bottle with our mouths in anticipation of the foam overflow that typically resulted. We then sauntered back to our bikes, sitting on the office curb, and watched the fascinating adult world go by.

When we weren't playing the games, we would play baseball games like "run-down", or take turns at hitting or fielding practice. When we tired of these, we would frequently get together for a baseball card trading session. The three of us started seriously collecting cards in the summer of 1969. Trips to the grocery or drug stores became adventures. We would collect our dimes together, and whoever was making the trip became our "buyer". Once the buyer's work was done, we would get together for an opening party. The wax paper coverings quickly flew off as we ripped open the card packs. We absentmindedly laid aside the sugary, stale pink slabs of chewing gum as we carefully leafed through the cards in each pack. The simple white-bordered photo on front contained a circle in the top right or left hand corner identifying the player and his position, and in yellow letters along the bottom of the card was the player's team. The pink reverse side of the card contained all the player's vital statistics, as well as a small cartoon noting some important accomplishment. Hope was always high that you would get either your favorite players or the few remaining cards to complete the current series. Once we took inventory of our collected "team", we would begin our trading session.

Our trading sessions never involved card price guides or assessment criteria for card quality. We traded to obtain players on our favorite teams, or to complete our series. I was a Mickey Mantle and Sandy Koufax fan, and so I collected all the Yankee and Dodger players I could. I traded many a future Hall-of-Famer for journey-man infielders who just happened to be wearing Dodger blue or Yankee pinstripes. Tony was a big Cleveland Indians fan, and he felt much as I did. To this day I still have some guilt when I think about the infamous Mickey Mantle for Richie Scheinblum deal. When we concluded our deals, we didn't carefully place our cards in protective plastic sleeves, but rather we tossed them haphazardly in a shoebox, and later stacked them into team piles and secured them with rubber bands.

When the other two thirds of the Suburban League were not available, I created my own games. I played rebound off the side of the house with a tennis ball. Having a paved driveway made for a fast but true surface for ground balls. It was like playing on black Astroturf. I would pitch entire games against the wall. I broadcasted each imaginary at-bat using my best Curt Gowdy voice, and artfully threw the yellow, balding tennis ball at the house at the exact position and angle to produce the desired outcome, be it a ground ball deep into the hole at shortstop, or a bunt down the third base line that the third baseman would have to bare hand. When my Dad noticed small splits in the white wood siding of the house, my rebound games came to a halt. He bought me a net rebounder, but it lacked the versatility that the side of the house produced, and the long grass of the backyard was no match for the true hops of the black Astroturf. We ultimately struck a compromise in which I could resume my tennis rebounding game along the side of the garage. Unfortunately the side of the garage was a mix of compacted dirt and gravel, and my fielding percentage quickly took a tumble.

Practicing hitting by myself was a bit more of a challenge, but I came up with a system. Our square backyard was fenced in on two and a half sides, with the garage enclosing the third side and the house completing the square. In the corner where the house joined the chain link fence, the round cement top to our well sat as the perfect home plate. The well cover was roughly in line with the tall maple tree that stood behind the opposite end of the house and next to the garage. The canopy of the maple tree spread wide almost to the house, and ran the length of garage. Our red swing set was roughly in line with the cement home plate along the "left field" fence line. Right about where shortstop would be was a tall ash tree, whose branches reached out broadly to almost touch those of the maple tree. I would take my 30-inch maple Rocky Colovito bat and three wiffle balls, and I would create and broadcast games just as I did in my rebounding game. Tossing the balls up in the air to myself (varying location depending on the strength of the imaginary opposing pitcher), I would take my best cuts.

My backyard field was a pitcher's park. Though the right field wall of the garage was short, its height and the interference of the canopy of the maple tree made reaching the garage roof (and hitting a home run) most difficult. While the left field line posed only the interference of the porous fielding swing set, the left field fence was too far for the wiffle ball to clear, even with a solid swat. The left center and center field fences were even further and also posed the problem of the ash tree, whose long branches gobbled up most fly balls. The only good field to hit to was right center field, where the fence met the end of the garage. The distance to the fence was reasonable with a good swing, and if you had the right trajectory on the ball, you could split the difference between the arms of the two trees.

I would go through the imaginary line up, switching sides of the plate depending on the hitter I was impersonating. I mimicked the batting stance of Red Sox outfielder Carl Yastrzemski, holding the bat high in the air, or that of Yankee outfielder Roy White, holding the end of the bat handle low and close to my belt. I faithfully replicated the pumping bat wind-up of Pirate first baseman Willie Stargell, and the fluid, looping stroke of Dodger outfielder Willie Davis. I went as far into each at bat (or inning) as the three wiffle balls allowed, then ran to collect them, returned to home plate, and resumed the hitting. I think I usually ran out of steam retrieving balls before nine innings were concluded, but most of the big name players I saw every Saturday in NBC's *Game of the Week* made their appearance in my backyard.

Indeed Saturday afternoons were reserved for the only game you could see on TV. Veteran play-by-play announcer Curt Gowdy and former Yankee shortstop and color announcer Tony Kubek brought you the *NBC Game of the Week*. I would get my bottle of Mountain Dew and my bag of pretzels, and I would sit cross-legged on the floor in front of our color Zenith TV. Usually sometime after my snack had concluded and the rhythm of the game had been solidly established, I would get out my baseball cards. I might sort them numerically within teams. I might try to replicate the teams playing of TV with my card collection. Unfortunately I rarely saw my favorite teams, as the Yankees and Dodgers were going through some lean times in the late 60s. The one exception was Old-Timer's Day at Yankee Stadium. Regardless of how poorly the Yankees were playing at the time, the draw of seeing the Yankee legends back in "the House that Ruth built" insured the *Game of the Week* would make at least one stop in the Bronx.

They were indeed halcyon times. Warm sunny days with boundless time and, for the most part, free of regimen or responsibility. It was before the onslaught of year-round organized youth sports, television with hundreds of channels, and computer games that do their best to replace reality. It was a time when imagination was more important than innovation, and wonder was easily found in the suburban world around you. It was a time when your excitement was limited only by your creativity and how far from home you were allowed to ride your bike. It was the dusk of simple childhood.

The crack of the bat was like a near-by thunderclap, and it abruptly woke me from my dream. My head quickly jerked up and to the left, following the flight of the grass-stained ball that had been launched like the Apollo space capsule sitting on top of a Saturn V rocket. I turned my body to watch the arcing projectile's reentry and descent, as it demonstrated a trajectory down range for the stand of Mulberry trees in dead center. The five fielders behind me stood in their tracks in a similar pose, bringing twelve eyes to bear on a sudden explosion of glass and flying of fur as the ball returned to Earth in the middle of the Arnold's front window. There was a brief moment when time seemed to stand still, and all became quiet and serene. The orange sky reflected off the shards of remaining window, and the lightning bugs began to glow. It was then I realized the stampede of fielders that began approaching. I stood staring incredulously as my team mates flew past me on a dead run toward the bikes lying haphazardly behind home plate and down the left field foul line. I turned to see the opposing team already mounting their bikes to ride off rapidly into the western sun. I glanced to my right to see Randy Sorrell slowly approaching. He had no distant haven in which to flee. We heard the clap of the Arnold's house trailer door fly open, and could see Mrs. Arnold's gray head pop out and gaze our way. We knew she could only see our shapes at best, given the light and the fact she was not wearing her glasses. Randy said, "Take off, we'll deal with it all later." I broke out of my spell of disbelief, ran to my bike, slipped my glove onto my handlebars, and peddled off.

THE SCRIBBLER CHRONICLES

I am, and always have been, a scribbler. It has always been my nature to, as the folks at American Heritage Dictionary might say, "fill pages with meaningless marks and lines." Now to be fair, the true nature of meaningful is relative. Each person's definition of what has value or significance can be quite variable. So to say my many marks and lines have been *meaningless* might be a bit harsh. While I'm sure that those with more refined tastes of language may find my marks less palatable (some might say vomit-inducing), I can say with conviction that at least a small audience of one found them quite valuable.

Filling pages with pictures and stories was vital to me. It started before I went to school. My Grandma and Grandpa Van Zant always provided my brother and I with drawing tablets whenever we visited their house. Armed only with long number two pencils with bright pink erasers (always in plentiful supply to support Grandma's crossword puzzle addiction), we would fill the pages of those books with pictures at amazing speed. Once a tablet had been completely filled on both sides, we qualified for a new one. The most common themes were depictions of war scenes, racecars, and spaceships, but occasionally rock groups, cowboys and Indians, and dinosaurs graced the pages. Sometimes there would be odd mixtures, such as dinosaurs and space ships doing battle. I'm sure to my grandparents it was just something to keep us busy and quiet, but to me it was a ticket to different worlds and emotions.

My love for filling pages with marks continued into elementary school. I got some "street cred" for my work until the fourth grade. Our class was asked to create drawings of Disney characters for stage decoration for the elementary school play. Large banners of butcher block paper were taped to our classroom wall, and a selected few "artists" in the class were given time away from regular class work to complete these commissioned works. Using storybooks as guides, we were each to depict our assigned character. I had the unfortunate luck of attempting to render Mary Poppins. No cartoon mouse, duck, or cricket, this was a real adult human women, and the picture I had as a guide was only a shadow figure in flight, her right arm extended securely holding her parrot-handled umbrella. To further complicate the task,

I had to make the scale transition from a quarter page book diagram to a banner twice my size. My fellow artist classmates who were lucky enough to draw Mickey or Donald or Jiminy were able to use the class projector to enhance their image and could almost trace their figures. "Where is the art in that?" I thought. When the class artists had finished the banner templates, the remainder of the class then worked on coloring the pictures. While our teacher Mr. Thompson praised all the completed works, I was sure that my disappointment in the drawing was shared by both him and my classmates. He was too classy of a guy to say anything; my classmates were not.

"It looks like a big fat blob with bad teeth," said one 10 year-old critic. While I could say that the British were not known for their oral hygiene, his cryptic description of the picture was on the whole quite accurate.

It was then I discovered that my marks and lines were really meant for me. If I tried to make something with the goal of pleasing others, it was sure to turn out to be just another fat blob with bad teeth. So I stopped trying, and went back to making the marks and lines for me. Later that year Mr. Thompson caught me drawing a battle scene from Rommel's North Afrika Campaign instead of doing the assigned English lesson. In addition to confiscating the work, he made me write a two-page report on the Field Marshal (in retrospect I must admit this was an excellent teaching method). For extra credit on a Science test, Mr. Thompson had us draw a plane, identifying all the essential parts. I drew a P-51 Mustang fighter escorting a B-17 bomber, and I'll be damned if I was going to ruin that picture by depicting where the propeller and ailerons were.

In fifth and sixth grade, I found a like soul in Brian Liby. Brian was quiet and thoughtful, had a dry wit, enjoyed science fiction, and loved to draw. We shared pictures back and forth for a while until we came upon the idea for a collaboration. It was the "Zoo of Madness". Basically, we would create mythical creatures of either terrible or ridiculous origins, and depict them as they might appear on display in a zoo. Each had a fictitious Latinized scientific name, and a brief description of the animal's unique characteristics. Sadly, the volume of over 100 animals is lost to elementary school history. Memory only allows me to recall Brian's elegant depiction of the "Huge Headed Little Bodied Pelican" (*Cranium largis pelicanus)*, complete with top hat and bow tie.

Probably as a result of reading John Lennon's *In My Own Write* and *A Spaniard in the Works*, I started becoming enamored more with words, and less so with pictures. An equally good reason was the fact that my artistic skills failed to mature as rapidly as I had hoped. I became fascinated in using words to tell funny and unexpected stories. Early works with such titles as "The Fable of the Magical Pith" thankfully no longer survive, but the following was the product of an assignment in eighth grade English class to write a Christmas poem. It was not selected as one of the best to be read over the school's loudspeaker before the holiday break, but that was all right, because it had been much enjoyed by the intended audience.

THE SAGA OF SANTA AND THE LABOR UNION

T'was the day before Christmas,
And things didn't seem right.
Christmas was only but one day away,
And Santa was in a dim hopeful light.

Some jerk had searched very deep,
Into the records he did seek,
To find U.A.W. facts,
On what the reindeer's contracts lack.

George Meany, president of the A.F.L.C.I.O.,
To Santa he did show,
The rights he had neglected,
That the Labor Department had selected.

Meany went to their crowded stalls,
And listened to their many heated calls.
"Poor housing, low pay, rotten plumbing," they did protest.
"What we need around here is rapid progress."

The elves had long since constructed and packed the toys,
That would soon bring happiness and many joys.
But the reindeer would be very much the key,
As they soon set up their Local 423.

Then the news went through the air like a shocking blight,
The reindeer voted to execute a wildcat strike.
Santa did not know what to do.
Who would fly him across the world? Who?

Santa knew there was only one step to take.
It was a step though, he would have to make.
He sent a wire to the commander-in-chief,
And told him of his latest grief.

Late that night, as fast as a flash,
The Senate and the House were in a mad dash,
To impose the Taft-Hartley act,
And get the reindeer back.

So this Christmas be thankful there are no presents you lack,
While Santa is drawing up a brand new contract.

This work began a kind of pattern. Because teachers had a way of assigning what seemed to be rote and arbitrary assignments, I saw it as a challenge to make it into something more imaginative. When told to write a theme about rain, I wrote a two-page story on how an emergency medical technician comes upon the scene of a horrific mountain road accident during an intense Southern California rainstorm. As he makes his way to the wrecked automobile, he finds the lifeless remains of his brother and his nephew. To my surprise, the teacher liked the theme a great deal. For freshman English in college, our teacher told us to critique a poem of our own choosing. I chose to provide a satirical review of John Lennon's "I am the Walrus", wishing to make fun of all the pompous literary reviewers that deem their opinions more important than the product.

"I am the Walrus," A Satirical Outlook

In 1967, John Winston Lennon, MBE, composed a song which he said was a satirical look at critics who told him what his songs meant. He stated, "Let them make sense out of that!"

Come now, Mr. Lennon! Do you believe that through this front you can hide the fact that the song "I am the Walrus" is the ultimate musical statement on the social life of modern man? One needs only a general understanding of the use of metaphor and symbolism to realize the true message of this musical and literary masterpiece about the human condition.

This seven-verse work is introduced by reverse guitar chords, symbolizing a reversal of man's musical ingenuity today. The opening line, "I am he as you are he as you are me and we are all together," obviously relates the belief that the people of the world are all joined in thought and deed in a transcendental dimension of time and space. This union of man exists far beyond the conscious mind.

The next line in the first verse, "see how they run like pigs from a gun see how they fly, I'm crying," is a metaphoric statement on the accelerated pace of human life today. We run about in our little world with the speed of a projectile, as do pigs in a crowded sty.

The concluding statement of the line mourns this condition by "crying."

The chorus, "I am the eggman, they are the eggmen – I am the walrus. Goo Goo Goo Joob," appears four times in the song and unites all the verse messages with a special cohesive symbolism. In stating he is an eggman, the poet is saying that he is a being of thought, fragile in make-up. He then includes himself in society (they are the eggmen) and states that the social order is going to die. This is achieved by taking the persona of society and appearing as a walrus (the sign of death in the ancient lore of many Mediter-ranean countries). The statement "Goo Goo Goo Joob" is an example of the reversion and downfall of man's societal order.

Two of the hardest hitting lines appear in the fifth verse. "Sitting in an English garden waiting for the sun" means that man awaits the heavenly salvation. This act is represented by the sun. In such a case, we can assume a darkening of such a light (a tan) must mean blissful death. The line, "If the sun don't come, you get a tan from standing in the English rain," can only mean man's self-destruction by a nuclear war. Radioactive fallout (rain) is to bring about death (tan) because a definite defensive position was taken. The defensive position is represented by the word "standing" as contrasted with the word "sitting" in the previous line.

These are just a few choice examples from this ballad of humanity. Lennon has pinned down the human condition with great accuracy. Such an insight should be investigated carefully so we may improve both man and the world he lives in.

Again to my surprise, it was well received, and was actually published in a collection of freshman compositions.

Another important lesson I learned was that scribbling helped me to explore my emotions. Always rather quiet and shy, marking pages was my way of shouting out. It was an outlet, though safe and silent. It was a way to "verbalize" my thoughts and emotions, and to question what it was that I truly believed.

This form of therapy first proved particularly useful in dealing with the emotional roller coaster that was my junior year of high school basketball. Growing up in Indiana, most kids are indoctrinated with the religion that is high school basketball. The activity serves as the tie that binds local communities together. The term "Hoosier Hysteria" is an accurate descriptor of the feeling. I had caught the fever on my own, as the rest of my family wasn't particularly enamored by "ball sports". The only problem was that, while my work ethic and passion for the game made me a coach's dream, my physical talent for the game was marginal. As so aptly reported by one of my coaches in a letter of recommendation for a high school award, I was "a very hard worker which makes up for the lack of natural ability that he does not have." I had played eighth and ninth grade basketball and junior varsity basketball to very mixed reviews the three previous years, and so when the varsity coach announced just weeks prior to the first game that I had made the varsity team, no one was more shocked than I. I felt this great conflict of excitement for being an Indiana high school varsity basketball player, and guilt for achieving something that, deep down inside, I didn't really deserve. I began to chronicle the season as a way working through these feelings. It ended up being a short story I called *A Season on the Outside*.

As it turned out, it was a season like no other. My high school team, the Blue River Valley Vikings, had been the perennial doormats of the county. This year however, returning most of the starters from last year's team with some talented new faces (myself excluded), expectations for success were high for the first time in ten years. Our hard driving head coach had carefully nursed these players through their development for the previous three years, and now he and the community expected to reap the rewards of their hard work and patience. We promptly went out and lost our first two games to weak opponents, and our coach unexpectedly resigned. At the time I wrote:

> We proceeded to our locker room, and sought anything to strike or mutilate to relieve our inward aggression. We all took our showers, dressed and sat down. Ominously, the air seemed dead. Mr. Foley had come down to us after the game, and subconsciously maybe we knew it was coming. Mr. Foley arrived and told us of his resignation of the job of head basketball coach. With these few uttered words, jaws dropped and eyes grew wide with amazement. Tony Goff (our senior star player), to whom Mr. Foley had been coach, teacher, advisor, father, and keeper, broke out in a flood of tears. Foley continued to tell us that he felt that we and him (or his philosophy) were not made for each other. He said Mr. Gardner, the assistant coach, would be the coach and practice on Monday would be as usual. All was in a state of confusion, sorrow, and wanting. We were all confused about the details and upcoming results of this action. We inwardly held sorrow for this man who had given so much to us and, with only two games into this young season, yielded to the challenge. Mostly, there was wanting. A wanting for something material and concrete to hold onto. Our pillar of authority was gone…As I walked out into the night air I stepped into a brisk winter wind. The wind seemed to represent the time ahead for us. Would we hold fast and press on, or would we, like a leaf, be blown into oblivion.

We ended up being blown around a bit, but ultimately held our own and worked to a winning season (quite an accomplishment for our little school). Along the way I injured my finger and thought I might miss the rest of the season (I fortunately only missed three games), talked the coach into letting me play both junior varsity and varsity, but found my playing time limited on both teams, and became something of a star (or oddity) in entertaining the team with fictitious play-by-play accounts of future games or leading bizarre sing-a-longs on the team bus following our road victories. At some point in time toward the end of the season, I started to see that the importance of a team was insuring that all the subtle, important roles were filled.

I didn't play varsity all weekend, and I played only sparingly for the junior varsity. It is hard to say you are pleased about not playing (to be honest, it is impossible), but it's just a facet of the game that is imperative. I view it as a role reversal. For those who sit bench, their playing time must be practice. Here is where their clutch free throw, last minute steal, or 20 footer at the buzzer will be realized. For all they do in practice makes those who do play that much more aware of their weaknesses. I can recall diving for a ball in the "bloody bucket" drill that I probably could have recovered conventionally, and was chastised by forward Roger Massengale for my hustle. But later in practice I noticed Roger hustling more than usual in another drill. I scored a big bucket for us that day, but it won't appear in anyone's scorebook.

The state tournament is the culmination of Hoosier hoops hoopla, and in 1975 the tournament was still a single class event where all schools, regardless of size, competed in the same tournament. The tournament began at the sectional level, with small local area tournaments of 6-12 schools. Our sectional was in New Castle (advertised as home of the largest and finest high school gymnasium in the world), and this would be my first taste of the tournament "on the inside".

I wanted the first step to be special. I was stepping into the Roman Coliseum and awaiting the blare of royal trumpets. With my coming, I joined basketball history. Actually it was just practice in the New Castle Fieldhouse, but to me it was a bit more some how. As I shot around, I pictured Muncie's Sam Drummer slamming one home, or New Castle's Kent Benson lofting a hook from the left baseline. It was a bit more real.

In this one case, even my practice experience could not hold a candle to the real event.

> That night anticipation was high. The air was heavy with excitement, and as we walked down the stairs to the gym floor, I knew this was going to be a rather "unique" experience. Upon entering onto the floor I saw that people were in the stands. That sounds like a rather stupid statement, but for some reason, I never really pictured people being here. During warm-ups I tried to look like I knew what I was doing, but I think most people realized I was scared shitless.

> For the line-up announcements I was first. I was really fired up and I went out to the center circle…and everybody else went to the free throw line. I'll never forget that. I felt like a real ass.

> Commentary of the game rather spoils the entire story. We played awful. With the exception of Tony Goff, who true to form as he had done for the past four years played a fine game, our starters couldn't hit the broad side of a barn. I played the last minute under direction from Mr. Gardner not to "mess around". We were in for a reason. One of my reasons was nearly put down my throat in the form of a blocked shot. My lone sectional claim to fame; an "almost" shot.

After the game the locker room was full of anger and remorse. Our Principal came in and told us we had a good year, and Mr. Gardner came to each us and told us a little something. Amidst curses and tears in the background, Mr. Gardner told me that I had really come a long way and that he thought I'd really help out next year. I kind of laughed inside, but I think he really did mean it. After the whole ordeal, I never thought whether there would be another year or not. I should have thought about that, but I naturally assumed there would be. In fact, I had the audacity to assess my playing chances. I guess it hit me. I finally belonged.

In the spring of 1976 my sister Cassie died. She was 21, and I had but a few memories of her. She was born with physical and mental handicaps that led to her being institutionalized when I was three years old. I only had memories of infrequent visits to the hospital which, as a child, I found both depressing and scary. One image I did have was a visit in which my Mom, brother and I took Cassie outside to enjoy a warm spring day. We sat around her wheelchair on the ground under the shade of a large oak tree, and she smiled and laughed with such a sweetness and purity that I will never forget it. Not long after the funeral, I wrote this in tribute to her beauty of spirit.

IN MEMORY OF CASSIE

Oh loved one, now the battle is over.
The long, lonely years in the bodily prison have come to an end.
Your teeming spirit and intelligence are now free to experience the world
where time stands still.

Oh brave one, you faced it all.
Though weak and frail and helpless, you possessed more courage in your heart and soul than anyone.

Your weakness created your strength.

Oh dear one, you were so very special.
Your touch was that of love itself,
and your laugh was like the finest symphony.
On that fine spring day, your smile filled the surroundings
with an essence of happiness.

Oh wise one, you are now to reap your reward.
Through your eternity of hardships,
you are now going to an eternity of happiness.
Though left behind there is a void,
before us there is a fulfillment.

In college my shyness led me to write a lot of poems for and about a lot of girls. Most were just pining epistles from a geeky guy with a bad complexion and without a cool car, but I rather liked the imagery of this one. It failed to impress the intended audience, largely because it was never shared. But it helped me work through yet another failed crush, and for that I was grateful.

CORNER OF JACKSON AND THIRD

The dense fog strangles the night
as it ominously slithers through the air.
The smell of the sea is thick,
and the muffled breakers echo far away.
The shapeless light from yet another lamppost looms behind,
and I once more enter darkness, alone.

The sharp, crisp clap of boots on the wet sidewalk
is the only sound betraying the solitude.
The stoic brick buildings hug close to the walk,
but they have long since died of loneliness.
My mind is still tormented with a whirlwind of thought,

and finding answers is like catching leaves in the cutting autumn
breeze.

A steady stream of rainwater rolls slowly along the pockmarked curb,
and is swallowed by an iron grid drain set amid the cobblestones.
All tributaries ultimately lead back to the source.
All thoughts ultimately lead back to her.
I can only explain how I feel by that thing called love,
but how can I be sure, for how can you explain that which you do not
know?

The grainy sidewalk is fractured and broken.
Time has walked heavily upon it, and pressure has caused it to crack
and divide,
constantly growing ever smaller.
Her image weighs heavily on my mind.
And though my mind may be divided as to my course,
my heart pleads to be heard and seeks to be one.

The shapeless fog curls around the light of the approaching lamppost.
As I am bathed by it's shining pool, I see below an unblemished
sidewalk,
and before me dimly shines the metal of a stop sign.
I have come down a long, dark, silent road.
It extends itself before me still, as I gaze forward into the misty
blackness.
But I grow weary, and here I want to stay.

I can't recall any particular event behind the following poem, but it was one of
my favorites. I got to thinking how life evolves into phases, like the changing
of the seasons, and each element of the environment takes on new meaning
during each phase.

CHANGING SEASONS

And in the spring the wind carries
the shrieking laughter of tiny people.
Ditches become vast canyons,
and grassy knolls grow to heavenly peaks.
The falling rain dances off the sweet supple face,
and the sun gives a dark forever friend.
All is new and exciting to the eye,
and the heart is a vessel of innocence.
Time is a thing to think little of,
for it is always there.

And in the summer the warm breezes
cool the sweat laden brow.
Ditches become ditches,
and grassy knolls obstruct the view of the next hill.
Falling rain means a day wasted,
and with the sun comes the toil of the field.
All is plain and blurred,
and the heart is a seething caldron.
Time is a thing to think little of,
for it forever drags on.

An in the autumn the cutting wind
violently fills the air with leaves.
Ditches obtain beckoning calls
and grassy knolls are seen as such.
Falling rain blurs images seen
through already distorted eyes,
and the sun gently warms a wrinkled face.
All is new and escaping,
and the heart grows weary and cold.
Time is a thing to think little of,
for it can no longer be captured.

And in the winter the gusty blows
chill the body with an ancient coldness.

Ditches become homes
cut into grassy knolls.
The falling rain sounds an unheard beat
while the sun shines brightly in black.
All is closed to searching eyes,
and the tattered heart is cold.
Time is a thing to think little of,
for it no longer exists.

Over the years, scribbling has continued to serve me well. Family births or deaths, marriages or divorces, moments of youthful exuberance or thoughtful aging contemplation have all been cause for filling pages with those "meaningless" marks or lines. In the process I continue to learn more about myself, and when all is said and done, that is the real value. It is therefore not important that, once these words are written on a page, they may ever once again see the light of day. In the writing, the purpose has been served, the joy has been extracted, and the meaning of these marks has been met.

THE DAD DIARIES

Bradley Scott and Kourtney Marie Van Zant,
Silver Spring, Maryland, Fall 1991.

Parenting is as old as life on the earth. Born literally from the biologic imperative to perpetuate the species, parenting has evolved into a mixture of art, intuition, and science. It is a role practiced with amazingly disparate skill and compassion. Some parents lose or relinquish any personal identity beyond that of parent, while others woefully neglect their role of provider and protector, sadly to the detriment of their offspring. As with most anything else in life, success often depends upon finding the appropriate balance of perspective. It is a perpetual pursuit that most any parent believes they will never quite "get it right". One thing is certain however. Parenting forever changes you. It is the rare person indeed that can remain the same self-centered human most of us are, after they have looked upon their son or daughter for the first time.

Because of this impact, much has been written about the joys and sorrows, ups and downs, and exhilarations and hardships of parenting. It seems each person finds his or her own way of coping. Faced with the prospect of fatherhood in my 29th year of life, I chose to write a journal to my unborn child. It was a way of sorting out my thoughts and feelings about who I was, what I valued, and how I was going to cope with this new role of "father". As a self-described "scribbler", it seemed only natural. I was finishing my doctoral degree classes in Kent, Ohio when "The Dad Diaries" began.

JANUARY 22, 1987

Two days ago our hearts jumped, our spirits were lifted, and our lives were forever changed: we discovered we are going to have a baby. And while its true that having a baby is a relatively common thing in society, it's also true that your first experience with parenthood is quite unique and special. Your reaction is a melding of almost every human emotion; excitement, joy, fear, courage, pride, jealousy. You're a prime example of emotional schizophrenia. Right now there is a great sense of anticipation in the air about everything. After all, your arrival is eight months away. We're just kind of getting used to the idea. To help me kind of sort out my feelings about all this, I thought I'd keep a journal of how we handled your development and arrival. Perhaps it will make for amusing reading for you one day. I don't know how successful this endeavor may prove to be. As Mark Twain said (or at least hinted at), the keeping of a travel journal or diary is a project of great folly destined to failure. I feel a great urgency however to corral a few of my galloping thoughts and feelings. Right now, our most prominent feeling is one of growing love. To be able to care for and love you will be fulfilling to our souls.

After you live with the secret for a while, you decide to share your joy. You also start to gradually see things, particularly babies, in a different perspective.

JANUARY 27, 1987

My parents called this evening, and I told them that your Mom was pregnant. They seemed kind of stunned, and not quite as excited as I thought they might be. Perhaps the news came too suddenly and abruptly. It was no time at all before your Grandpa was talking about cars or IU basketball. You'll find that Grandpa is not the most expressive guy. It's difficult for him to open up. Unfortunately, I think I'm too much the same.

JANUARY 31, 1987

We went to a Broom Hockey Party tonight at Dr. Lemon's. The Lemons have a five month-old daughter, and one of the guests had a four month-old son. Needless to say, I was much more attentive to the young ones than I would normally be. They seem so fragile, but I know they are quite resilient...like the human spirit itself. They represent an unfilled vessel, a piece of stone awaiting the master sculptor. Their potential is so vast. To think I will be responsible to help fill this vessel and sculpt this stone. I pray I will be up to this responsibility. Forgive the sober tone; you'll find your Dad gets too serious about things sometimes. Maybe you can help me loosen up a bit!

FEBRUARY 13, 1987

Well, the humbling nature of keeping an updated journal is beginning to catch up with me. A lot has transpired since my last entry, but time has been drifting away from me.

We received a letter from your Uncle and Aunt early this week. I wrote to them last week to announce your discovery. It was a difficult letter to write. They are in the process of adopting a child, and I thought (rightly or wrongly) that they might feel a little sad with our announcement. I believe they have been trying to start a family for a while. Their adoption process seems quite lengthy, and I thought that our joy might only emphasize their emptiness. Their letter back was a happy one, and they wished us well. They said their adoption home survey will begin in April. I hope all goes well, and soon we will both be experiencing this "parenting thing". Perhaps if one of you gets overly tedious, we could trade off for a while!

My parents are going to Florida today. They called Wednesday, and sounded much more excited about the pregnancy. I think they have gotten over the shock. Your Grandma Van Zant said Grandpa and Grandma Diekman (her parents, my grandparents, your great grandparents) were excited, and she said Aunt Marian (my Great Aunt, Grandma Diekman's sister) and Aunt Marie (Great Aunt, Grandpa Diekman's sister) will be "beside themselves".

We've been reading stuff right and left about parenting, babies, breast feeding, etc. We went to the library, the doctor gave us a lot of materials, we picked things up at the hospital, and people out at your Mom's school have given her stuff to read. And I know it's only begun! I'm finding out a world of interesting things, such as, "did you know that an infant's stool may be yellow or green in color with the consistency of a tar-like paste?" Sounds like we'll be in for some good times!

We started a name list last weekend. Your Mom has been much more prolific than I. Boys names seem more difficult to "attach to" than girls names. I wonder how fair it is to decide on a name before we see you. I mean, what if we decided you just didn't look like a "Winston" or an "Ellenor" upon arrival. (Not to fear, we'd never name you Winston or Ellenor.) As I told your mother, we've got a little while to decide still. Hope our selection meets your approval.

Upon our first doctor's visit, I began to chronicle (and study) fetal development, keeping a running commentary on the changing events, as well as the changes it seemed to have on me.

FEBRUARY 13, 1987

February 5th marked our first visit to the doctor. Dr. Carol Foote put us very much at ease. She is young, bright, and very open. You're about ten weeks into your development. Dr. Foote tried to listen for your heartbeat "just for fun", acknowledging that it was a little early yet. We went to the hospital for your Mom's blood tests. It's kind of a small hospital, but seems relatively modern. I guess it will be as good a place as any to enter this world.

MARCH 3, 1987

This past weekend, we went to see the movie "Hoosiers". It was about a small 1951 Indiana High School basketball team achieving something special, fighting against substantial odds. As a past "Hoosier Hysteria" warrior, it was quite a nostalgic trip. Since the film was shot in Indiana (some of it shot in Henry County), it was quite stirring to see scenes from your memory up on the screen.

You'll find I'm quite a nostalgic kind of guy. I sometimes wonder if I've been misplaced in time. I cherish the memories of youth: summer days riding my bike down to the park to play baseball, evening runs down silent, narrow country roads, hours spent "shooting hoops" in the driveway. While you must always look ahead and live your life today, it is pleasant to briefly relax in the past.

You'll also find that I tend to worry more than I should, especially about money. There is no particular reason I should be so overly conscious about money. We never really wanted for anything we really needed. It's strange. I worry about you, too. Will we give you the kind of home you deserve? I think we can do it; I know we have the love. We are going to do our best. I worry about your Mom. I know she would rather stop working to stay home with you longer. However, with me in school, she is the breadwinner currently. It's tough on both of us, but hopefully it won't be tough on you. That's not to say we won't have to deal with pain, tough knocks, hard decisions, and occasional heartache. It's all part...sometimes an important part...of growing and living. It's all of what makes us what we are. Hopefully, we can help you through the tough times. That's what family is for. Our families have meant a lot to us. Sometimes we don't always see eye to eye, but they are always there when needed.

I hope this hasn't sounded to preachy. (Your Mom says I have a bad habit of lecturing. Maybe you'll feel the same!) I certainly don't claim to have all the answers, but I know I do have a few more answers than you will, simply by my 29-year head start of bumbling through life. My only recommendation: make the most of every minute. Life is a gift: give thanks and cherish it. Enough said, end of lecture!

MARCH 5, 1987

Our second visit to the doctor gave us our first physical experience of your presence...a heartbeat. Via fetal sound monitor, we heard the rapid (160 beats / min) thumping of your tiny heart. A chart in the doctor's office told us you are now about five inches long and weigh about one ounce. There was a great sense of wonder hearing your heartbeat. We came closer to a new, developing being. Before you were just a thought and the reason that your Mom's pants were no longer fitting.

My parents got back from Florida Monday, and they called Tuesday night. I think they are getting quite excited about the idea of grandparenthood. You will be the first grandchild on both sides of the family. It may prove to be a difficult situation, but I certainly don't think you will lack for attention.

APRIL 4 AND 5, 1987

It has been a busy day. We have been getting ready for Tim and Amy's baby shower. Tim is the newest faculty member at the lab at KSU, and he and Amy have become good friends. They are expecting in the middle of the month. It is really nice to be going through this parenting thing with friends. We had six inches or so of snow today. We have also had sleet, freezing rain, rain, and about any other form of inclement weather possible. Ahhh, nothing like spring in Northeast Ohio!

Our four-month visit to the doctor went well. Your heart rate was 160 beats / min and your positioning in the uterus was as expected. Your Mom has been very tired, and her back is starting to bother her more. Well, I think I must cut this short and get to bed, since we lost an hour going to daylight savings time today. I'll close with a phrase we anticipate you'll hear most every day of your life...we love you!

APRIL 17, 1987

Today is Good Friday. It was overcast this morning, but the sun came out beautifully this afternoon. We are slowly making preparations for your arrival. Last Friday your Mom brought home some clothes she bought from a person at work. There were so many cute things. I don't know if she knows something I don't, but she bought several older girl's outfits. This past Monday, Tim and Amy had a boy. Tim said he hasn't slept all week, but that it has been the greatest thing that has ever happened. He said he couldn't quite explain it, but it was well worth it. I look forward to your arrival with some trepidation, admittedly. I'm unsure of myself, really. But more and more, the excitement of your arrival increases. Your Mom says I'll be a good father. I can promise you I will do my best.

Today we bought a crib. It's going to take a bit of sprucing up, but I think it will be OK. I still need to paint your room. It will be hazy blue with white trim. Hope you like it. I will close now. The Easter holiday, a traditional time of rebirth and renewal, will take on a special meaning this year. We love you very much.

APRIL 25, 1987

Yesterday we went to the doctor to get an update. At about five months, you weigh about one pound, and you are about one foot in length. Your Mom has felt you move. I think I felt a little rumble, but I'm not sure. I'm sure in the weeks to come, your movements will be much stronger. That prospect will be quite exciting. Next Friday, your Mom is scheduled for an ultrasound. It will be your first picture. Not exactly Olan Mills, but it will be beautiful all the same. Don't forget to smile!

Last Tuesday, not long after we first felt your movements of life, was the birthday of my late sister, Katherine Ann Van Zant. Cassie would have been 32 years old. She passed away in 1976. She suffered from microcephaly, which left her with a broad array of birth defects. She lived most of her life in the New Castle State Hospital. It is one of the greatest disappointments of my life that I didn't have the courage to know her better while I was growing up. She had one of the brightest smiles imaginable. I think only my Mother loved her as she deserved, and maybe even she didn't fully understand her and the situation. I wanted you to know that your late Aunt was a beautiful person; a treasured soul held captive in a crippled body. Knowing her has forever changed my life, and I will always remember her. She gave me a greater capacity to love. I hope we can pass a similar gift to you.

MAY 1, 1987

Yesterday, we saw you for the first time. We saw your heart vigorously beating, and we even saw you 'rub your nose'. It was exhilarating to actually see you move. I was at a loss for words.

I just finished watching the move Hunter. The 1980 film was the last of the late Steve McQueen. It was the story of one of the last bounty hunters, whose girlfriend of eight years is about to give birth. McQueen's character is uncertain about his role as prospective father. A friend recalls that a Chinese philosopher once said, "A man is nothing more than his family." The recycling of your life is exciting, and gives you the feeling of a common life thread through time. As George Harrison once said, "It's all too much."

That may not make a lot of sense now, but at 2:00 am, you can't expect much. I'm off to bed.

MAY 7, 1987

I've been meaning to get this entry in for several days. I felt you move officially Sunday (May 2) afternoon. There we were, sitting on the couch, watching the Bucks/76ers playoff game, and your Mom told me to feel her stomach, because you were kicking. She had been feeling your kicks for a couple of weeks, but I had not yet noticed them. Only a few seconds had transpired before you gave an inspired kick. I was so surprised, I instinctively pulled my hand back. My eyes lit up, and I took a deep breath. Your Mom about lost it; she thought I was so funny. Late that evening while in bed, I felt you kick several times. Your Mom says it feels like being poked, only from the inside. It's times like these that, in a way, I almost envy your Mom. She has that special bond with you. For me, it's kind of like being on the outside looking in.

MAY 17, 1987

Well, today marks the ending of my twenty-ninth year. I can hardly imagine the challenges and changes before me in this one year ahead of me before I turn a score and ten. We had a splendid brunch at the Silver Pheasant. The man that seated us told of his experiences with the births of his two sons. He told me to make sure I was there when the baby was born. For him, the births of his sons were his most exciting moments. I assured him I planned to be there.

I've been trying to picture the scene 29 years ago. When I came into the world, Eisenhower (a heroic general of World War II) was president, and TV was just becoming a household reality. The Cold War was reaching a peak. You'll be coming into a world which sees Ronald Regan (a former B-movie actor) as president, the VCR is becoming part of family life, and a supposed, but questionable détente exists between the US and the USSR.

Is this progress? I'm not sure. I can be sure you'll be entering a loving family that will do what we can to help you to a full and happy life.

MAY 22, 1987

Today marked our six-month visit to the doctor. Your heart rate was 152 beats / min, and your Mother's stomach measured exactly as expected. The doctor said all is well. At this point, you weigh about 1 ½ pounds. Your Mom has gained a total of 13 pounds. All is on course. Tonight we travel back to Indiana for the Memorial Day weekend. It will be nice to see the family, even though it will be hectic.

JUNE 13, 1987

I must admit, there have been several occasions when I've wondered if being parents now was a wise move. After all, I'm still in school, and our family's major wage earner, your Mother, will be out of work for at least four months. Money may get pretty tight, and I'll be getting to the point of finishing my research project and taking my comprehensive tests. I could be a real headache to live with (more than usual)! I guess there is never really a perfect time to start a family, though. They say if you wait for the perfect time, you'll never have children. I guess my anxious feelings are normal, though. As Father's Day approaches, I find myself reflecting on the responsibility and rewards of parenting. I have a good feeling about the institution. I can't promise you I'll be the best Father in the world, but I will promise you that I'll give my very best effort toward that goal. I hope you won't be disappointed.

After living with the evolving idea of becoming a parent for six months or so, you have experienced enough to come to terms with things. The doctor visits, the background reading, the input from others (both solicited and unsolicited) start to form an idea in your mind that, yes the day will be coming and, more than likely, you can handle it.

JUNE 21, 1987

This weekend your Mom has been tired, coughed quite a bit and had some trouble breathing normally. We laid down on the bed and tried to relax, and bantered about names for you. At one point I took out my latest issue of Sports Illustrated and went through most every page, placing most every name within the magazine up for nomination. Your Mom vetoed most by adding the middle name "Moe" to the selections. In the span of an hour, she was feeling much better. She and Thomas (one of our cats) napped while I stayed up to watch the late movie (Harry and Walter Go to New York). As of now, we like the girl's names "Courtney" and "Karleigh", I favoring the former while your Mom favors the latter. Boy's names seem to be much harder to come by. I think your Mom believes my choices for boy's names are much too plain. I promise you though, that upon your arrival, we'll think of something…and I doubt if it will be Moe, so don't fret!

JULY 12, 1987

Well, I've been quite remiss in keeping up with my correspondence with you. Your Mom's family was up over the weekend of the 4th. They are very excited about your upcoming arrival. When I asked your Grandpa if he thought he was old enough to be a grandfather, he quipped, "I think I am, but I'm not old enough to be married to a Grandmother." Your Uncle Brad is quite beside himself. (I always wondered where that expression came from…trying to picture a person "beside themselves"…Oh well!) Brad is quite a special guy. As a mentally handicapped young adult, he views the addition of a baby to the family from the point of view of a child. We kidded him about whether he will be an "uncle" or "aunt", depending on your sex. He has commented about how at first he wanted nothing to do with changing your diapers, and now he's looking to find someone to teach him how to change diapers. All this seems the more unlikely when you see this mixture of wonderment and confusion coming from a 6'4", 200 lb, 23 year old. But though Brad may frequently bring one to a point of exasperation, his love for his family, especially your Mom, is sure and strong. They have this special bond, and I think that's why she favors the name Bradley for you if you're a boy.

July 8th marked our first Lamaze birthing class. Lamaze is a procedure of controlled breathing and relaxation techniques employed to reduce the pain of delivery. These techniques, when coupled with patient education, help to take much of the fear out of the birthing process. The class has a large number of couples, coming from all backgrounds and walks of life. Many have had children before. Some have lost their babies through miscarriage. While you never want to think about such things, you wonder how parents handle such emotionally devastating experiences.

The first class basically was an overview of the birthing process…fetal development, physiological changes during pregnancy, and the baby's trip through the pelvis and eventually out into the world. As the instructor explained, it all seemed so simple, but yet so strikingly complex; a series of physiological changes that encompass a plan that is most perfect.

Your Mother thinks you have oriented yourself head down now, and she thinks she has had some false labor pains. All seems to be normal and quite on schedule.

As the night wears on, I should really take leave from this note and go to bed. A busy week lies ahead. I think the busy schedules and the hot and humid weather have made us both a little cranky, and less than at our best. I think after your Mom finishes her summer school this week, things will get better. Rest assured we are diligently preparing a place of love for you. Sweet dreams dear one.

July 31, 1987

Time is passing by more quickly than seems possible. One month and three days until your due date. It hit us this week in Lamaze class. Things are starting to seem a little more concrete. Realizing it would be normal for you to arrive two weeks before the due date, we realize we've got to get some things wrapped up. I've got to paint your dresser and put up your curtain rods. Your Mom has some sewing she needs to get done. Last weekend, we went "Back Home Again" to Indiana. It was really great seeing everybody, but the time goes so fast and the running to and fro can get to be quite tiring. Everyone back there is so excited about your arrival.

AUGUST 5, 1987

Today was quite eventful. About 11:00 am, your Mom noticed that you hadn't been moving quite as much as usual. Since she seemed worried, I told her to call the doctor. The nurse at the office had your Mom come in for some fetal monitoring and gave her a kick sheet to keep track of your activity. The monitoring turned out normal (as Dr. Ferrara confirmed when he called your Mom later in the afternoon), and the kick sheet seems OK. You're in a definite head down position, so I guess you're perhaps getting a bit edgy to get out. Don't rush on our account, though. We've still got a few things to get wrapped up. We took a tour of the maternity ward in our Lamaze class tonight. They have some nice birthing rooms. We hope we'll have the opportunity to use one. I get more and more excited (and perhaps a bit more worried) as things get closer. I hope we will give you a wonderful start in life, for you certainly deserve it. We'll do our best, but be patient with us. After all, we're only rookies at this!

AUGUST 20, 1987

Last weekend proved quite eventful. Friday night, Tim and Amy hosted a shower for us at their house. There were quite a number of people from the lab there. God, even Dr. Sinning was there! That's a surprise, because when we had a shower for them in April, he refused to come because he felt that men shouldn't be at baby showers. Tim joked that he told him it was a "social gathering". The folks at the lab chipped in and got us a stroller. It is a real nice stroller, and it converts into a carriage. I think you'll like it. On Sunday, we had a picnic for the Adult Fitness Program. Tim had us pick up the chicken, and when we arrived, we saw they had gotten together and chipped in for a gift. They gave us a second car seat and Bill Cosby's book Fatherhood. We have been very fortunate with all the kindness and generosity we have received from people we have only known a couple of years.

Tuesday your Mom went to the doctor for a non-stress test. They recorded your heart rate, and she recorded each time she felt you kick. The doctor said everything looked good. We go to the doctor again tomorrow.

AUGUST 22, 1987

Yesterday, Dr. Foote said that you've dropped down. Your Mom has been feeling some pressure / pain in the groin…a sure sign of labor soon to come. When Dr. Foote told us that "…if you make it to next week…", we really realized that time is indeed growing short.

I finished up Bill Cosby's book Fatherhood. It was a pleasant reading. He spoke of his trials and tribulations as an experienced father of five. He also stressed that parents are not perfect. He himself has made 6, 937 mistakes…and is counting. We will make mistakes too. (After all, we are rookies.) There will be times when we will seem the most stupid people alive; that we won't be fair and won't understand. Well, all of those may be true (except the stupidest people in the world part…after all, you have to cut us a little slack), but what will always be a given truth is our love for you. Right or wrong, our intentions will be only for your best interests as we see them. You may not agree with them, but I hope you never doubt our sincerity of purpose toward you.

Finally, the day arrives.

AUGUST 30, 1987   9:57 PM

Today marked your beginning, Bradley Scott Van Zant. Around 4:00 am, your Mom started feeling weak contractions and noticed some discharge of fluid. She thought her water had broken, and she was well into labor, since the contractions were now only two minutes apart. We both weren't sure though, since the contractions were so weak. She called Dr. Foote at 7:00 am, and she instructed us to come to the hospital.

By 8:00 am, we were in a birthing room, and labor officially began. Dr. Foote broke your Mom's water and verified that the amniotic fluid was merconium stained. This yellow/brown tint to the fluid meant that, at some point in the pregnancy, you became distressed (such as lacking oxygen due to impeded blood flow through the cord) and released waste (i.e., pooped) into the fluid. This automatically made you a more high-risk baby, and it was therefore decided that you would be delivered in the delivery room.

The morning passed away slowly, one contraction at a time. It started out rather easy, but by late morning your Mom was really in pain. She received some Demerol that took the edge off the severity of the contractions. Her progress was "painfully" slow up until about 1:00 pm, when one of the nurses relieved your Mom's bladder. The added room allowed you to quickly descend.

The same nurse (I think her name was Sharlotte) served as a great supporter for our Lamaze breathing and relaxation. Your Mom had been breathing great, but too fast. She was also too tense. (I guess we should have practiced a bit more diligently.) She and I helped your Mom to relax, and progress came fast. Your rapid descent also resulted in an unusually precipitous drop in your heart rate. The nurses turned your Mom away from the monitor, and gave her oxygen. I was very worried when the monitor showed a heart rate of 78 beats / min. You recovered quickly, and before we knew it, Dr. Foote had arrived and we were 8-9 cm dilated.

Your Mom fought the urge to push for a number of contractions, puffing vigorously into the oxygen mask. She was on her side most of the time at this stage because she felt some strong back pain. You see, you were turned face up, which usually puts more pressure on the back of the pelvis.

At last, she was allowed to push, and push she did. Once you started to appear, we went down to the delivery room. The plan was for a very controlled birth, allowing you a slow entry into the world so the stained amniotic fluid could be suctioned before you cried and aspirated it into your lungs. That was the plan. In reality, even though your Mom "puffed through" the contractions, you quickly popped out, crying not long after your delivery.

Quickly you were taken to a warming table and suctioned. I leaned over kissing your Mother through my bulky surgical mask, telling her that we had a beautiful boy. The look on her face was a strange cross of abounding joy and utter exhaustion. After you were suctioned, foot printed, tagged, and given eye drops, your table was wheeled close to the delivery bed. Your Mom gave a finger to your little left hand, and you grasped it tightly. I rubbed your chest and played with your right hand. You gave an occasional vigorous cry, but for the most part, you stared up at us (or at least in our direction), your lower lip quivering from the relative chill of this new world. I thought about what you must think…out of a dark, warm, aquatic world and into a bright, cool, airy environment. What a trauma to the system!

We held you for about one half hour in recovery. Even with all the dried blood and vernix all over you, you were the most beautiful thing! Your head was so well rounded, and full of dark, curly hair. I held you for a long time, gently rocking and swaying you back and forth.

10:57 PM

Well, the actual day has been chronicled above. It was surprising, frightening, physically and emotionally trying, and exciting. I think I've been running on adrenalin most of the day. Now, as a family, much lies ahead for us. Ours will be like any other family. We'll have our pride and pain, our joys and sorrow, our pleasures and our hardships. But we will always return to a central theme. Through it all, we must use our love and trust as a common thread to keep things together no matter what the weather brings into our lives. Sleep sweetly tonight, young man. We love you dearly.

The journey was over, and my son and I could now talk face-to-face, and no longer needed the pages of a notebook. The diary was summarily tucked away, and the work of learning my new role of father began in earnest. About two years later however, I found myself rifling through boxes in search of the notebook, for a new correspondent was on the horizon.

SEPTEMBER 14, 1989

My apologies for not addressing you sooner. I'm afraid you might find that your Dad has been, and will continue to be, quite busy. I'm working on my Ph.D. (hopefully I'll eventually end this continuous student trek!) and need to get everything wrapped up in a couple months because I have a job in Maryland, and you and your Mom, me, and your brother Brad will be moving in December. Should all go well, you'll make your scheduled appearance on or about March 7, 1990, somewhere in Maryland.

There is much to tell you, and little time to do it. Over the next few months, I'll try to relate a bit of what goes on in my mind as you are growing. Years from now, it may give you a sense of history... or a few good laughs!

For tonight, I will say only that you were conceived in Kent, Ohio in June, and are about three to four months along (We'll know a few more specifics tomorrow, for your Mom goes to the doctor). Though Mom is teaching (Special Education), and I'm writing and teaching (Exercise Physiology), and Brad is keeping us both quite busy at home, we are very excited and happy about the thought of us being a family of four. I hope you will be equally pleased with us. Unfortunately, you have no choice. I'll do my best to be the best Dad I can be for you. You deserve no less. Good night dear one.

Life sometimes has a way of overwhelming us, and the demands of the world wear away until we sometimes think we hardly have time to breathe. And yet, if we're lucky, we step up to the plate and keep the inning alive. That was the situation that we were certainly in, just like the mode of operation of most young families. As a result, my dialog with my young correspondent was brief, but perhaps as a result, a bit more introspective. The stolen moments of correspondence were those rare moments available to think outside the ever-present whirlwind of the ordinary world.

SEPTEMBER 18, 1989

Well, I finally got both Brad and Mom to bed (the former was much more difficult), so I thought I'd finish my ritual evening snack (cereal and coffee) with a few words to you. Doctor's report is... you're fat! Dr. Foote said your Mom was a bit big for this far along, and she was surprised that Mom had felt you kick already. Your Mom will have an ultrasound done Tuesday to check things out. We'll get an opportunity to see you... kind of an indirect first meeting.

If all goes well, they will be able to measure the length of your developing skeleton, and confirm how far along you are. Your Mom has been very tired this weekend. I guess having a two year old and being pregnant really takes it out of a person. It sometimes makes us wonder how our friends with three or four kids do it.

I spent much of the afternoon going through apartment listings for Maryland. I hope all the upcoming changes won't be too much for you and Mom. I think she is worried about leaving. I can certainly understand, but we'll need a full time income once Mom delivers. I think it will be OK. It may be tough at first, but I have a feeling it will all work out. It's 10:41 pm right now, and early morning fitness program awaits. I've got to go. I'll kiss you goodnight, and pray we all find peace in the months ahead.

September 25, 1989

Sorry to get back so late to you. The news is that you are just one and not two. The ultrasound last week said everything was OK. They thought you were either further along, or were really two people. As it turns out, if measures are to be believed, you are actually a couple of weeks behind schedule. We saw you do some kicking and waving; very impressive show!

This past week, one of the biggest hurricanes (Hugo) in memory slammed into Charleston, SC. Several deaths, hundreds homeless, hundreds of thousands without power. It really makes you think about how lucky we really are. We have home, health, food, and family. It is sometimes easy to forget the gifts, and to get greedy. That is something I hope you will always remember. Even when times are tough, and there will be some times that will be very tough, remember the blessings. Primary among those blessings is a family that loves you.

October 17, 1989

Greetings dear one. Today we went to the doctor, and heard your heartbeat; strong and steady. Dr. Ferrara said you and Mom are right on schedule. Brad has been saying hello to you. He'll stroll up to Mom, pat her on the stomach and say, "Hi baby." At first, he was a little confused and would say

"Hi baby" to my stomach. I think he has caught on now. Today I worked hard on revising my manuscript. I'm due to get it to the committee by Friday. This semester is speeding by. We've also been working on getting housing and doctor information in Maryland. A friend of mine from old graduate school days who lives in Maryland sent us some doctor names. Between graduation, moving, new job, and your arrival, the next five to six months are going to be wild. But we'll all get through it, no worse for the wear, one day at a time.

OCTOBER 19, 1989

Awoke this morning at 5:15 am to go to the lab and was greeted by the season's first snowfall. Winter beckons! Tuesday night, Brad and I sat in front of the TV to watch the third game of the World Series (Oakland A's lead San Francisco Giants, 2 games to 0). Four minutes into the pre-game, the picture went to static, as commentator Al Michaels began to utter the word "earthquake." When communications were restored to the city about one half hour later, San Francisco was ablaze and severely shaken. Two days later, the death toll has reached 297. Many were killed as the top of Highway 880 collapsed on the lower level. Amazing reports of survival of a few fortunate survivors of the collapse are joyful yet gruesome.

OCTOBER 29, 1989

Today Mom and Brad went trick or treating…his first excursion. We found some Mickey Mouse sweats with ears on the hood. I raked leaves and put a second coat of paint on Brad's "big guy" bed. We need to get him comfortable in a big bed before the move, so that is one less adjustment he'll have to make. I gave the manuscript of my dissertation to the committee nine days ago. Hopefully, Wednesday will be the day I defend it. If successful, that will be the last step (short of handing in the final copy). It has been a long road, and there are times when you wonder if it is all worth it. They say you can't go wrong with more education. Well, I've run the gambit and I'd agree to a point. What's really important is what you do with that education. Will you make a difference? It is my sincere hope that I will.

NOVEMBER 5, 1989

Well, it has been a busy week. On Wednesday, November 1, I defended my dissertation…the last official test for the Ph.D. degree. All went relatively well. I've got some revisions to make, but I should be able to get it all wrapped up in time. Friday morning at 5:20 am we set out for Maryland to find a place to live. We found a house to rent that may be a bit expensive, but should prove a comfortable home. I think you'll like it. Things might be a little tight, but rest assured we'll never be short on love. Your Mom has been having some serious heartburn, but otherwise is OK. We are collecting names of doctors in the Silver Spring area. I'm sure we'll have a doctor and hospital lined up by March 20 (or thereabouts).

NOVEMBER 19, 1989

Today I handed in my last copy to the printer. Things are now winding down. Today we went to a "memorial party" for Gert Parmenter, the long-time technician at the lab. She passed away last week of cancer. I must say, I found this means of remembering a departed loved one to be novel and warm. It made you remember all the good times. I think that's good for the grieving process.

The last two weeks have served to change the political landscape of the world. The world in which you and Brad will live may be radically different from the world your Mom and I experienced. After 28 years, the symbol of East and West division, the Berlin Wall, has fallen. Berlin is now an open city. Following the lead of the Soviet Union and Poland, all Eastern Europe (except Romania) is opening up their economies to Western ideas. Democracy seems to be awakening. I hope this new mood will serve to bring the world a little closer together. We could all use a bit more understanding.

NOVEMBER 21, 1989

"A rose by any other name would smell as sweet…" Your name is the one possession that is solely yours; one that no one can take from you. For that

reason, the pressure is on us to give you a name you like. Your brother ran around day-care today saying "Karleigh". This is a name that Mom is lobbying for. I favor Courtney. Now, if you are a boy, who knows what your name might be. I like Derek. Personally, my guess is you are a girl. A friend of ours in Muncie thinks you're a boy. Supposedly, she has a great track record in predicting the sex of babies. Mom thinks you are a boy. I had a dream about a boy before your brother was born. No baby dreams yet, but I'll keep you updated. Boy…girl…it matters not. We have enough love to go around. As long as you're healthy, we will consider ourselves most blessed.

NOVEMBER 27, 1989

Today was the first Monday after the Thanksgiving weekend. Thanksgiving is the holiday where we pause to give thanks for our many blessings. Tradition holds that the early white settlers of North America held a feast with the Native Americans in celebration of a good harvest. Traditionally, our family goes to my parents for lunch, and later to your Mom's family for supper. We had the usual splendid repast. We enjoyed family conversation, watched a little football, and Brad and your cousin Katrina (five days younger than Brad) had a great time playing. It just strikes me how blessed we are. Oh sure, we have our problems. But when all is said and done, we are safe, feed, warm, and loved. You can never overestimate the importance of that last component.

DECEMBER 3, 1989

Late Sunday night, and Mom and Brad are in bed. Just thought I'd write you a line or two to say hello. It snowed a ton today. It was pretty, but it was not so pretty as I was shoveling it this afternoon. Mom worked on some cross-stitch, and Brad would have gone out had we been able to find his boots. I can only imagine how crazy it is going to get in the coming weeks. Mom's heartburn seems a little less severe, but she still gets tired pretty quick. I hope she (and indeed all of us) holds up well underneath the burdens of the move. I'm sure it will all work out. We put the Christmas tree up Thursday, and finished decorating it today. I especially enjoy the tree now. The light glimmers in the dark, and the snow outside reflects the light of the street lamp. All is quiet and peaceful. Sometimes the simple times are the very best. I hope we may share many together. Love to you...good night.

JANUARY 6, 1990 FROM SILVER SPRING, MARYLAND

Though it may have seemed like it, I really haven't forgotten you. The past month has left little time to write you. In addition, once we got here, it took a while to find which box our notebook was in. We've got it together now, however. Since we last talked, I received my Ph.D., we celebrated Christmas with my family, we hosted a "going away-end of the semester-Happy Christmas" party, we loaded up all our worldly possessions in a 24 foot truck, we moved to Silver Spring in sub-zero weather, we celebrated Christmas with your Mom's folks, rang in the new year by going to bed early, and I am still waiting to get officially hired by the US government. In general, we have all fared well. Your brother seems to have tolerated the move quite well. Your Mom had elevated blood sugar at the last doctor visit in Kent, and so she has been on an 1800-calorie diet to guard against pregnancy-induced diabetes. She had the same initial test reaction with Brad, but an extended hospital glucose tolerance test showed she didn't have a problem. Mom had a similar test done before leaving Kent, but we haven't heard the results yet. She found a doctor here in Silver Spring, and you all have an appointment on Tuesday. We are now about two and one half months from "D-day" (delivery day), and doctor visits will now be about every three weeks till about two or three weeks before your due date, then visits will be each week. Well, it's late, and we have early church tomorrow. We tried the Methodist Church close to home last week, and will visit again tomorrow. So much has happened, and many more changes are going to occur. But as long as we trust in each other, we will be OK. I love you.

FEBRUARY 2, 1990

Happy Ground Hog's Day! It's a quaint little custom where a fuzzy mammal in Pennsylvania predicts the weather for the next six weeks. I know it doesn't make sense; you'll find that a number of things in this world don't necessarily make sense. The ground hog didn't see his shadow, so we are to have an early spring. We'll see. It's almost been a month since we last talked. I started work January 16th, and things have been OK there. I've been working overtime to build up some leave time, so I can take some time off when you're born. We've had two visits to the doctors, and all is going well. Your Mom's blood glucose was OK. Your heart rate was 140-150 beats / min last visit. Your next visit is next Tuesday. With about one and one half months to go, we are trying to get it together. Mom broke out Brad's old clothes to start preparations. We'll be getting the bassinet out. Mom is checking into buying cloth diapers. Though it doesn't seem like it now, I'm sure we'll be ready. I believe you will find your brother quite interesting, annoying, and caring. He may find having a new "center of attention" hard to get used to. There will be times when the two of you may be at each other's throats, and you may think Brad to be the strangest soul on Earth. But you should know that he loves you very much. For a couple of weeks now, he's been saying "kiss a baby and make it smile". I await with excitement, and admittedly some trepidation, when the three of us become four. It should be a wild time.

FEBRUARY 17, 1990

I'm writing you from my desk at the lab. I went in this fine, sunny Saturday morning to get a little extra work done (and to build up a bit of credit leave so I can take some days off when you arrive) and remembered as soon as I hit the light switch that there was a power shut down on "the farm" today. So for the past hour and a half I've been doing some deskwork by the sunlight streaming through the window. It would be a most pleasant and quiet time, were it not for all the equipment buzzers going off every few seconds.

This week has been one of sadness. The minister of our church, Rev. Edward Van Metre II was killed in an auto accident on Monday. We had only met him in person twice, but we had listened to him preach several times. He struck me as a highly motivated, open, caring man; the kind of person this world couldn't afford to lose. He was vital, healthy, and filled with a great zest for life. He leaves behind a wife and four children. We went to the viewing Thursday night at church. Hundreds of people were there to pay their last respects; true testament of his impact on this congregation. Brad was very patient. I think he understood that something was going on with all these people, and yet such a quiet scene. It started me thinking about how fragile life is. Too often we take for granted this, our greatest gift. It is good advice to periodically step back, reflect, and understand all the good things our lives have to offer. In the face of adversity, there is always the hope of a better day. I know when I see you for the first time, I will be thinking of great gifts, and hopes, and the wonders that this life can bring.

MARCH 5, 1990

Good morning! Thought I would write a few lines here at the lab before things get busy. Saturday we toured Holy Cross Hospital; the stage for your first appearance in the world. We have heard some good things about the hospital. Our friends, Mark and Julie Walton, had their little girl (Molly) there, and they had a good experience. Your Mom has met all four doctors that comprise the OB/GYN practice, and all seem really nice. She especially likes Dr. Ann Burke (the one that you visited Friday of last week). It would be interesting if she delivered you, since Brad was also delivered by a female doctor. You may say, "Why is that so unique, since roughly half the people on the Earth are female?" I would say that, "Society has been slow to evolve past certain stereotypes of what men and women can and can't do." Traditionally, the "women's place was in the home," while the man "brought home the bacon." This kind of hearkens back to the hunter and gatherer days when males, generally being physically stronger, foraged for food while the women kept warm the home fires. In the United States in the late 20th century, there is not a lot of hunting and gathering to do, that is if you don't count trips to the grocery (which can be an ordeal in and of itself sometimes). Women are now equally capable of fulfilling most any job that was traditionally restricted to men. That is not to say there are *not distinct differences, both physical and social, between the sexes (which can, on occasion, make for a much more interesting world), but in general women are just as capable of performing a particular job as a man. Societal change is slow however, and in some ways that's OK. That may be sexist, but it is hard to fight off thousands of years of social mores in a single generation. Well, best get back to work. Your scheduled arrival is but 10 to 15 days away. I'm not sure if we're ready, but we'll do our best.*

MARCH 15, 1990 9:16 AM

A little more than five hours ago, at 4:14 am, the world became a little warmer, a little more exciting, and a little more loving. You came into the world with little protest, considering the trauma of entering a dry, cold world full of light; a totally opposite environment to what you've experienced since conception. Mom had been actively pushing through three contractions when you appeared face down (normal position). Dr. Anne Burke took your head and turned you slightly as your shoulders emerged. Dr. Burke then suctioned your mouth and nose, and you uttered your first sound. The remainder of your purplish, vernix-covered body quickly followed your head and shoulders, and you were placed on your Mother's chest. Dr. Burke clamped your umbilical cord, and gave me scissors to cut your last link to your past world. A bright but exhausted smile came to your Mother's face. Your lips quivered. Nurse Debbie tightly wrapped you in a blanket, and Mom and I just stared at you...so beautiful. Like your brother when he was born, you have a plentiful head of black hair. Your face and limbs are fuller than Brad was, but you are a bigger baby; 8 lb. 15.8 oz. (Essentially 9 lb., but knowing how women historically are especially aware of their weight and age, we won't burden you with the extra 0.2 oz.) Nurse Debbie took you over to the bassinet to clean you up a bit, and did APGAR scores. She than swaddled you tightly in a new blanket, put a little stocking cap on your head, and gave you to me so I could hold you. Oddly, I was a bit hesitant for an instant, for I thought I needed to be gowned to hold you, but I quickly cradled you up and gently rocked side to side with you. As I held you, your lips opened and you stuck out your tongue. (Hopefully not a subjective opinion of Dad at such a tender age.) You even started to open your eyes a bit. The lights were obviously very intense, and the eyelids quickly closed. I handed you off to your Mom, got the camera, and took a "team picture" of you, Mom, Nurse Debbie, and Dr. Burke.

It all started at about 5:00 pm yesterday. We were in Brad's room (I should say Brad's and your room.), and Mom and Brad were sitting on the bed. I had just gotten home from work not too long before, and was watching Brad kiss his stuffed bears. Mom leaned forward, paused, and suddenly yet calmly announced that she thought her water broke. This means the sac of amniotic fluid in which you were floating had ruptured. This meant that, by hook or crook, you were coming into our world within the next 24 hours. Mom called the doctor's office, and Brad and I ate supper, and got his bag ready. Mom received instructions from Dr. Burke (she was on call), and finished packing her hospital bag. We called Mark and Julie Walton about watching Brad, and I got Brad dressed. Somewhat begrudgingly, Mom and son parted company and I took Brad to Walton's (to see Molly!) for the night. I told him we were going to the hospital, and that he would have a baby to visit with tomorrow. I kissed and hugged him. I don't know if he has any idea what's going on. We will soon see. Upon my return, Mom had pretty much finished packing, taken a shower, and was getting dressed. I straightened up the house, closed the windows (we had been experiencing an unseasonably warm streak…up into the mid to high 80's), and put a load of laundry in. By 7:15 pm or so, we were off to Holy Cross Hospital (about a 5 to 10 minute drive away).

We went straight up to maternity following a brief stop at the emergency desk. (A women with a stomach the size of a small medicine ball whose water has broke and whose contractions are two minutes apart commands attention!) We camped out in birthing room number five at about 7:50 pm for the beginning of a long and fatiguing night and morning. We watched "Night Court", "Dear John", and "Quantum Leap" as the contractions became increasingly stronger. Your Mom's previous high spirits were slowly waning, but she remained strong. I think it was sometime during "Late Night with David Letterman" that the pain and fatigue simply became too much, and your Mom got an epidural (form of anesthetic to lessen the pain of contraction). Not long after that, your heart rate dropped, and we turned you and Mom to the side and put Mom on oxygen. This is not an uncommon response to the epidural, and it wasn't long before your heart rate returned to normal. Once the epidural kicked in, Mom and I were able to rest about one and a half hours. Contractions then became stronger as the epidural wore off, with the discomfort getting intense enough to warrant another anesthetic dose. It was about then that Mom felt the urge to push. Nurse Debbie was going to have Mom do some "easy" pushing, but the crown of your head was in ready view. Dr. Burke was then called, and the prologue to your life in our world was complete.

March 15th begins the first sentence of a novel that will hopefully be filled with many wonderful, amazing, happy, and loving moments. There will hopefully only be a few passages of pain, sadness, and woe; but remember that these are a necessary part of any meaningful story. As your parents, we are charged with the task of setting the stage, supplying the background and the foundation. With God's help, we will be successful, and you will have the tools you need, and the bulk of your story will be written by you. You will have the skills to meet all the challenges, grasp the opportunities, and make the moments your own. Remember however, that you always have a loving family at your ready support. There will always be an ear to listen, a hand to hold, and a shoulder to help carry the load. We love you dearly.

I tucked the diaries away, for we were now busy living the history of a newly minted family of four. As I foretold, we experienced wonderful, amazing things along with painful and sad things. Ultimately we became a family divided, and then a family blended. But through it all, we never lost the love. The love had indeed provided the thread necessary to sew our pieces together, and ultimately to keep our family whole.

SHARING A LONG OVERDUE CUP OF COFFEE

Playing at the park with my sister, New Castle, Indiana, August, 1992.
From top to bottom are Ellen, me, Bradley and Kourtney.

I held the quarter in front of the coin slot, the receiver cradled between the left side of my face and my shoulder, and the slip of paper with the name and phone number in my left hand. As the dial tone wailed in my ear, I gave serious thought as to if I really wanted to make this phone call. Things were awful tough right now. I was out of work, and the research job in Boston that I was counting on fell through. My wife had left me and took our two kids five months before, and I was holding out hope that by some miracle our family could be salvaged. I had moved back with my folks three months ago, and was making what little money I could now substitute teaching. Did I really want to open up a new personal mystery right now?

I was probably thinking that the way my life was going at the time, I needed something new; something that might shake the cobwebs out of my heart and jump start my brain. Maybe I was thinking that by making that call, I might find out something about myself; something I could hold onto. I dropped the quarter in, heard the clink of the coin in the phone, and started dialing the number on the paper. As it started ringing, I quickly rehearsed a salutation in my head. Suddenly a soft and sweet female voice said, "Hello?"

Not quite done with my mental rehearsal, an awkward silence blossomed for a moment before I was able to blurt out, "Hi, this is Scott Van Zant; I'd like to speak to Ellen Johnson, please."

It was only about ten years before, when I was almost 25, that I even knew she existed. One day when I was visiting my folks, Mom sat next to me on the couch in their small living room and said, "I want to ask your opinion about something." I thought it would be something like she was planning to paint the walls, and what color did I think she should choose. In the same matter-of-fact voice that you might use to discuss paint color, she told a story of how my Dad had been briefly married before he married my Mom, and how after he and his first wife broke up, a girl had been born. A girl my Dad had never seen until recently. She had made contact with my Dad about a year before, and (much against the wishes of the girl's mother) they had met a couple of times to talk. Those brief meetings had gone well for both of them, and she wanted to visit him at home, and maybe even meet his wife.

"Do you think I should met her?" my Mom asked.

My response was delayed, as I was still processing all the details of her story. Suddenly little subtle mysteries were falling into place. I remembered as a kid noticing the name "Pat" drawn in the top of the cement supports for my Grandma Van Zant's clothesline. I asked her who Pat was, and she said matter-of-factly that it was a friend of my Dad's, and dropped the subject. I remembered a story my Grandma Diekman told of reading the engagement announcement of my Dad to somebody while he had been dating my Mom. I could still hear her raspy voice chuckle in the back of my head saying, 'I turned to your Mom and said, Say Ann, aren't you dating this boy?'

I mentally shook my head, returned to the moment, and said, "Well, how do you feel about it?"

"Well, your Dad says she's real nice. I guess if she wants to meet, that would be alright."

That meeting and many others over the next few years went well for them. Not long before I moved back home, Ellen had written in a card she had sent to the folks that she would be interested in meeting her "brothers" if we were comfortable with that. Between weekend visits with the kids and the occasional day of substitute teaching, I had a lot of time on my hands to think about things. Trying to mentally and emotionally navigate the stormy seas in which I found myself adrift, I thought some piece of solid land to grab onto was a good idea, even if it was uncharted territory.

There had been many times I thought having the advice of an older sister would have helped greatly in trying to understand that other half of humanity.

I thought having that family female perspective might have saved me much embarrassment, heartache, and grief. Unfortunately I only had the briefest memories of my older sister Cassie, for she was institutionalized in the state developmental hospital when I was about three years old. I never remembered her in our home, and had just brief memories of visits we made at the hospital. Most were just seeing her lying in bed; maybe recognizing Mom on a good day. The one memory I treasure was one warm day, taking her outside in a wheel chair, sitting under a big oak tree, and seeing how happy she was to just be outside and feel the rays of the sun kissing her face. She was the picture of true joy and happiness, and that is how I will always remember her.

And now, after 34 years, I was going to meet my older sister for the first time. We had agreed to meet at The Waffle House in Muncie for an afternoon cup of coffee. We briefly described ourselves to each other over the phone so we would have a rough idea of who we might be looking for. She would be the short and somewhat thin brunette, hair about shoulder length, wearing round, wire-rimmed glasses.

It was a day in May with cloudless blue skies as I was driving north on State Road 3 in my eight-year-old blue Volkswagen Jetta that was pushing 100,000 miles. As the rich brown furrows of the newly plowed fields whisked past my car windows, I was racking my brain for things to say. What is the appropriate icebreaker in meeting your adult sister for the first time? Outside of having the same paternal origins, would we have anything more in common than any other two total strangers on the planet? Arriving a little early, the teacher in me jotted a few notes on a pad as possible conversation points. I got out, locked the car, took a deep breath, and walked inside the Waffle House.

Once inside, I quickly scanned the surprisingly crowded room and, by some strange magic, our eyes locked almost instantaneously. As I walked toward her booth, I noticed a warm glow emitted from the eyes behind her glasses. A similar glow beamed from the broad smile on her face. As I drew near, she began to stand.

"Hi, Ellen?," I said, raising the tone of the last syllable to inflect a question to which I was pretty sure I already knew the answer. Her smile seemed to grow even bigger, if that was physiologically possible, and she threw her arms around me saying, "Hello, brother."

We held an embrace that would have been much to long for strangers, but seemed just about right for siblings.

We sat down, and the waitress brought us two glasses of water, two cups, and a small carafe of coffee. After pouring our respective cups, I stared at her and, surprisingly, the words came like water tumbling over a falls. I had no need for my crib sheets. We were like distant classmates at a reunion, even though we had no common experiences. How could it be that I felt so comfortable sharing with this stranger I had just met? We caught each other up on our life stories to date, noting graduations, jobs, marriages, births, divorces, and our Dad. He was the strange focal point of two disparate lives that in all likelihood would have never crossed paths. But a high school girl's interest in her past, nurtured over the years against her mother's wishes, led her to wanting to meet her Dad...my Dad...our Dad. I don't recall how long we talked, or much of the specifics of our conversation. What I do recall is how easy and how natural it all was; and how weird that all seemed.

Later that summer before I moved to Arizona to start a new teaching job, she joined me and my kids for a small goodbye party at the park. We played on the slides and swings, and had snacks on the picnic table. We took family pictures, and like any big sister, she made horns with her fingers above my head. We had only known each other a few months, but we were as comfortable as if we had known each other for years.

Without a doubt, that was the best investment of a quarter I ever made.

DRAWING PICTURES FOR MY KIDS

Fantasia Mickey by Brad and Dad, Flagstaff, Arizona, November, 1993.

As we begrudgingly broke our embrace, tears came to the eyes of my four year-old son as I was struggling to hold back my own. His mother's hand gently fell upon his right shoulder and herded him to her side, joining his two year-old sister who clung to her mother's left leg. Their mother gave me a smile, seemingly much more intended for herself than for me, as I waved goodbye and slowly descended the concrete steps of the old brick Tudor home. In two days I would be packing all my worldly possessions that I could fit in my 1984 Volkswagen Jetta, and then driving 1,500 miles off into the Western sun. In the process I would be further away from my kids for a longer period of time than I had ever been before, and I wasn't sure how I was going to survive.

Divorce was breaking up my family. And while I knew my decision to leave was the right thing to do, not only for the financial support of my kids but also for my long term emotional health, I struggled with the problem of how to fill the void that the three of us would be feeling over the chasm of the many miles and two time zones. The first night on the road I wrote them a postcard from Chandler, Oklahoma. The second night, another from Gallup, New Mexico. I tried to select pictures that were colorful or cute; images that might appeal to toddler temperaments. But I quickly decided this wasn't the answer. These foreign images would likely have little appeal, and I could not be sure how my message would be translated to them through their mother's filter. My first month in Arizona I tried phone calls, but my autistic son had a mortal fear of talking on the phone, and the conversation skills of a two year-old are meager at best. Though not the answer, they would have to serve at least as placeholders; evidence, poor though it was, that I was somewhere thinking about them.

The best answer was unfortunately not possible. I knew "face time" was the answer. Time to be silly together. Time to read Dr. Seuss. Time to cuddle. Starting a new teaching job and a new life precluded being able to do much of that. I was looking forward to the Christmas break before my first class began. Early in the fall term I started making plans to present at a conference in the

East that would also coincide with spring break, thereby being able to have the school fund my face time. Imperfect solutions at protracted intervals, but my only option.

My work served to occupy my mind and my time, filling the gaping hole inside of me. I also resolved to make the most of the beauty around me. I increased my running, seeking peace amid the fields of wildflowers and towering Ponderosa pines. I met two people at the new faculty orientation, Karen and Anne, and we made a pact that the five of us (including Anne's husband Stephen and their dog Popeye) would go hiking someplace new every weekend. Little did I know that what I originally had envisioned merely as a means of solace would actually be my salvation.

The red Toyota Corolla jerked hesitantly up the gentle slope of the university parking lot, causing the red and blue graduation tassel hanging from the rear view mirror to dance back and forth. Karen laughed as my excessively serious demeanor got the better of me. How ridiculous was this? I was a 34 year-old father of two, learning to drive a stick for the first time, being taught by my girlfriend of two months who just learned herself this summer, when she bought the car. In fact, she had to enlist the assistance of two friends to help drive the car to Arizona from Lawrence, Kansas. At times, they drove as a team, one steering and pumping the clutch on demand while the other shifted into the appropriate gear. Life with Karen was new and exciting, always an adventure. Our weekly hikes had evolved into romance, with plans to drive back to the Midwest to visit our families over the semester break. That was, assuming I could get the hang of the manual five speed.

Heavy snow was flying through the mid-December morning sky as the Corolla chugged East. Having successfully graduated from Karen's driving school, I climbed behind the wheel at Gallup, and motored with relative ease along the lonely ribbon of I-40 stretching across western New Mexico. Our itinerary would include a stop in Lawrence to visit Karen's old friends from grad school (and to catch a Jayhawk basketball game at "The Phog"). We would then visit each other's families over the holidays before returning for the new semester in the New Year. Anticipation welled up inside of me. In such a short time around Karen, I felt alive once again, sharing things with her that I had never shared with anyone. Sometimes, I felt guilty because she made me so happy. I should miss the kids more I thought. I didn't realize that slowly, ever so slowly, I was starting to heal.

With the exception of nearly running out of gas in the desolate blackness of eastern New Mexico the first night of our trip, the ride home was a joy. With each passing mile we learned more about each other, settling comfortably into each other's life. By the time we reached Indiana, I had not only gotten pretty good at the stick (even surviving a major traffic jam through downtown St. Louis), but I had also gotten pretty settled in love.

Christmas with the kids brought a dizzying mix of emotions. Excitement upon being reunited after a four-month absence. Fear about whether they would recognize me after a four-month absence. Happiness in holding them close. Sadness in bending down to kiss them goodbye. On the way home I stopped at Memorial Park, and standing alone at the top of the sledding hill of my youth, with a bright pallet of white stars filling the inky night sky, I gave thanks. It had been exactly one year ago that I had stood in this exact spot, and wondered what my future would hold, and how I could survive it all. Somehow I not only had survived, but I had thrived. A year ago my dream had died, but now a different dream was taking shape. And while it was at one time hard to accept that new chapters in our lives required new characters and story lines, now the prospect of new characters and new plots was exciting. And while I had to accept that my role as Dad would be forever changed, I was resolved to make the best of the new story we would write together.

Sunbeams pierced through the majestic wall of stained glass of the historic, red sandstone church, creating miniature rainbows in the sparsely populated sanctuary. Karen's ten year-old niece littered our path with rose pedals as we walked toward the altar. As we approached the pew where my family sat, my son, seated next to the aisle, stuck his hand out to shake. Instinctively I reached out and shook his hand gladly. It was as if he understood how much I needed him to be a part of this moment. It not only was a blending of families, but also a blending of tangible remains of past dreams to images of new ones. While I had never been a believer in signs, there was something very moving and powerful about that innocent handshake; one that I will always remember. It was indeed a good sign. As Karen and I faced each other, gently holding each other's hands, I gazed into those eyes that had transfixed me just a year ago, and I could see her face beam, rivaling the rays streaming through the window at the back of the sanctuary. It was another good sign.

A few days later, Karen and I took the kids to Denny's for breakfast. With family and friends helping to celebrate, it was one of the first times the four of us were able to be alone together. As we sat in our booth, looking out at the deep blue morning sky behind the green Ponderosa pines, my son turned over his paper placemat, picked up a black crayon, and started making a series of circles. I thought little of the activity, and continued talking to Karen about the day's plans. Before long I glanced over once again, and noticed he had started a second series of circles, but these were in groupings of three, with two circles above and one below. Inside the bottom circle were marks that roughly approximated eyes, nose, and mouth. Below the circle clusters were a series of long, flowing strokes that resembled the pine needles on the trees outside. He had quietly drawn six of these figures. When I asked him what he had drawn, he said, "Mickey Fantasia." This was the first time I had ever seen him draw something distinct and concrete; something from his own mind that he wanted to share.

The next morning at breakfast, Brad took a red crayon in hand to the back of a new placemat, and he started the circles once again. This time I got into the act. I drew a pointed wizard's hat, complete with red stars and moons, on top of the head circle and nestled neatly between the ear circles. Brad finished the face, and drew two vertical lines down from the head that represented "Mickey Fantasia's" body, and finished each with circular flourish at the end designating his feet. I filled in the robe with more stars, moons, and planets. It was magic for both of us. It was then I realized I had found a connection. Pictures were his passion. I was committed to making them mine.

In the beginning, the projects were modest. I might draw some mountains at the bottom of a letter to show how the new snow looked on top of the San Francisco Peaks in October. I would draw a picture of what the aspen leaves looked like as they changed from their summer green to their fall gold. I might find an interesting picture of Mickey Mouse or Snoopy in the comics or a magazine, and I would replicate the picture in my own hand, and send it off for their enjoyment. It was then I began to realize that what I had started for their enjoyment had really become my own. For it was during those stolen moments from my hectic adult world, while making those pictures, that I not only felt closer to them (even though they were oh so many miles away), but I also felt closer to the their joy of childhood. I remembered the fun I had as a kid, loosing myself in different times and places while scribbling in the notepads given to me by my grandparents.

My evolving excitement in the projects spurred on my creativity. I began writing "picture letters", in which I would replace most of the nouns with pictures. It was fun crafting letters that could be adapted to this format and to my sometimes-limited artistic abilities. One Halloween I took used computer printout paper from school, and made a Jack-o-Lantern poster for the kids. With a fire roaring in the wood burning stove, and a stereo full of mellow

CDs playing in the background, I unfurled the continuous sheet ream with the holes running along each border onto our oak dining room table, and sketched out a huge pumpkin in the center. Arched above in "scary-type" lettering was "Happy Halloween Bradley and Kourtney". I then carefully outlined the sketch with a black art pencil, and spent most of an orange art pencil on the pumpkin. A colorful array finished out the lettering, and I signed "love, dad" in the bottom right hand corner. Before I knew it the evening had passed, the fire in the wood burning stove was merely glowing embers, and the stereo had given up the evening long ago. From these humble beginnings, a poster passion was born. Christmas brought an oversized "Santa Mickey". Woody and Buzz Lightyear implored them to "Fly into the New Year and Beyond". Snoopy and the Peanuts gang were hunting Easter eggs. The Fourth of July was heralded by "Uncle Mickey". In each case, the above poster creation ritual was happily repeated.

Holiday visits were always cherished time, for this was an opportunity for the all too rare "in person" connection. Usually far to brief, they were packed to the brim. Movies, Christmas family dinners featuring the traditional "shrimp cocktail eating contest", and summer trips along the Ohio River or to Michigan and Wisconsin were golden treasures to me. I usually had the added benefit of adding to my ever-growing collection of original artwork from Brad. While the subjects were usually rather limited (Mickey, Pooh, or other cartoon favorites), the joy was in watching the master at work. I can recall coming back from Michigan with Karen and the kids, sitting in a roadside diner, when Brad asked Karen for a pen so he could draw while waiting for our order. He asked for requests, and my selection was Garfield. Unlike me, who needs a model for most any character I draw, Brad calls up all his characters by memory, and began with the most central element; the nose. He gradually worked out with whiskers, eyes, ears, and lastly head. Before the food arrived, we had a perfectly proportioned Garfield for our viewing pleasure during dinner.

Between the pictures, the picture letters, the posters, the holiday visits (and the picture albums of those visits that I created for the kids), we made the connections. And though they were not the connections I originally had in mind when I became a father, given the circumstances, they worked. The two year-old turned into a young girl who became quite adept at talking on the phone. Even the four year-old boy got to the point of tolerating *brief* phone conversations. Eventually email channels were established, and the patterns for more mature connections were now in place.

Outside of the art collection I amassed over those years, the simple pictures I created are forever lost; fleeting images of memory. But they will always hold a dear place in my heart, for they created a connection that not only spanned the miles, but also spanned the years as well.

Afterword

The true treasures of history lie in the events of the everyday. The advancement of our society depends less on the words of leaders and the power of armies, and more on the bread of the baker, the safety provided by the public servant, the inspiration of the educator, and the love given by our family. This work sought to celebrate those "big and little incidents" that supported the feelings of five generations of "players". Billions of similar histories could and should be told. It is only then that we will truly appreciate the complex tapestry of humanity. And if we are able to gain even a glimmer of that appreciation, perhaps we will see those around us in a different light. Perhaps we will see that, when all the labels and bravado are stripped away, we are all more similar than different, more united than divided, more of a "whole" and less of a collection of "parts".

When all is said and done, the history of players is universal. Regardless of their time, place, or talent, players do their best to get by, and hopefully make the stage a bit more inviting for those that will follow.

CAST OF PLAYERS

Workers at the Heller Brothers Nursery, New Castle, Indiana, circa 1905.
Van Zant family members include Frank (third from left), Carl (fifth from
left), Charlie (eighth from left), and George (immediately in front of Charlie)

NICHOLAS VAN ZANT

Born: 1833, Ohio, United States

Died: Apr 1875, New Castle, Henry County, Indiana, United States

Father: John VanZant (1798? – 1834)

Mother: Nancy (Runyon) VanZant (1805 – 1860)

Siblings: Abraham (1825 – 1844), Catherine (1828 – 1913), Eunice (? - ?)

Spouse: Sarah Ann Reed (1833 – 24 Dec 1900)

Married: 12 Oct 1854

Children: Eunice (? - ?), Viola (1855? – 1886), George Austin (1857? - ?), Carl Ira

Profession: Carpenter

Nicholas Van Zant

CARL IRA VAN ZANT

Born: 15 Sep 1861, New Castle, Henry County, Indiana, United States

Died: 5 Aug 1944, New Castle, Henry County, Indiana, United States

Father: Nicholas Van Zant

Mother: Sarah Ann (Reed) Van Zant

Siblings: Eunice, Viola, George Austin

Spouse: Katherine Hood (29 Sep 1862 – 16 May 1940)

Married: 10 Feb 1883

Children: Lottie (23 Jul 1886), Frank H. (1890 – 1972), Charles R. (1890 – 1969), Clara, George Aaron, Alice (1898 – ?)

Profession: Factory Worker

Carl Van Zant, circa 1905

CLARA VAN ZANT

Born: 16 Jan 1894, New Castle, Henry County, Indiana, United States

Died: 14 Oct 1911, New Castle, Henry County, Indiana, United States

Father: Carl Ira Van Zant

Mother: Katherine (Hood) Van Zant

Siblings: Lottie, Frank H., Charles R., George Aaron, Alice

Spouse: Jesse Freel (1889 – 1930)

Marriage: 29 May 1909

Children: Jeannette Freel Van Zant (29 Nov 1909 – 19 Jun 1971)

Profession: Office Worker

Clara Van Zant, circa 1910

George Aaron Van Zant

Born: 29 Sep 1896, New Castle, Henry County, Indiana, United States

Died: 5 Aug 1973, New Castle, Henry County, Indiana, United States

Father: Carl Ira Van Zant

Mother: Katherine (Hood) Van Zant

Siblings: Lottie, Frank H., Charles R., Clara, Alice

Spouse: Marcella Mae Hessler

Marriage: 29 Sep 1924, Knightstown, Henry County, Indiana

Children: Robert George

Profession: Fireman and Fire Chief, Deputy State Fire Marshall

George A. Van Zant, circa 1925

MARCELLA MAE HESSLER

Born: 9 May 1904, Milhousen, Decatur County, Indiana, United States

Died: 12 Nov 1986, New Castle, Henry County, Indiana, United States

Father: Andrew Adam Hessler (1879 – 1949)

Mother: Catherine T. (Enderleine) Hessler (1874 – 1948)

Siblings: Aurelia R. (1902 – 1990), Angeleen M. (1907 – 1999), Marietta M. (1908? – 1986?), Cressy George (1910 – 2000)

Spouse: George Aaron Van Zant

Married: 29 Sep 1924

Children: Robert George

Profession: Nurse and Homemaker

Marcella and George Van Zant, circa 1925

ROBERT GEORGE VAN ZANT

Born: 16 Apr 1926, New Castle, Henry County, Indiana, United States

Died:

Father: George Aaron Van Zant

Mother: Marcella Mae (Hessler) Van Zant

Siblings: none

Spouse: Lou Anna Diekman

Married: 13 May 1951, Rushville, Rush County, Indiana

Children: Ellen Johnson (1950 –   ), Rex Alan (1953 –   ), Katherine Ann (1955 – 1976), Robert Scott

Profession: Postal Carrier

Robert G. Van Zant, 1944

ROBERT SCOTT VAN ZANT

Born: 17 May 1958, New Castle, Henry County, Indiana, United States

Died:

Father: Robert George Van Zant

Mother: Lou Anna (Diekman) Van Zant

Siblings: Ellen Johnson, Rex Alan, Katherine Ann

Spouse: Karen M. Gerhart

Married: 20 Nov 1993, Flagstaff, Coconino County, Arizona

Children: Bradley Scott (1987 –), Kourtney Marie (1990 –)

Profession: Teacher

Scott Van Zant, Flagstaff, Arizona, 1992

FREDRICK H. DICKMAN

Born: 18 Jul 1819, Germany

Died: 03 Jul 1900, Shelby County, Indiana, United States

Father: Henry Dickman (? - ?)

Mother: Johanna Dickman (? - ?)

Siblings: unknown

Spouse: Catherine Miller (? – 1858); Johanna F. Lorenz (22 Jun 1834 – 09 Sep 1909)

Married: 1847, Columbia, Pennsylvania; 12 Dec 1858 Hamilton County, Indiana

Children: Barbara (? - ?), Emilie (? -?), Henry (? - ?), John A. (? - ?), Catherine M. (? - ?), Frederick W. (? - ?); Maggie M. (? - ?), William T. (? - ?), Anna M. (? - ?), Frank T. (? - ?), Matilda L. (? - ?), George C., Bertha (? -?)

Profession: Shoemaker, Farmer, Homeopathic Physician

Fredrick and Johanna Dickman

George Conrad Diekman

Born: 06 May 1874, Shelby County, Indiana, United States

Died: 08 Jun 1935, Richmond, Wayne County, Indiana, United States

Father: Fredrick H. Dickman

Mother: Johanna F. (Lorenz) Dickman

Siblings: Maggie M., William T., Anna M., Frank T., Matilda L., Bertha

Spouse: Catherine Eberhardt Klund (19 Mar 1876 – 14 Sep 1945)

Married: 1895, Shelbyville, Shelby County, Indiana

Children: Marie Anna (01 Dec 1896 – 04 Dec 1999), Carl G. Diekman

Profession: Baker, Farmer, Cabinet Maker, Factory Worker

George and Kate Diekman with Marie Anna, circa 1898

CARL GEORGE DIEKMAN

Born: 25 May 1902, Shelby County, Indiana, United States

Died: 28 Mar 1995, Indianapolis, Marion County, Indiana, United States

Father: George C. Diekman

Mother: Catherine Eberhardt (Klund) Diekman

Siblings: Marie Anna

Spouse: Margaret Marie Ballard

Married: 04 Dec 1920, Newport, Campbell County, Kentucky

Children: Carl Junior (1921 –), Lou Anna

Profession: Baker

Carl Diekman, circa 1920

MARGARET MARIE BALLARD

Born: 11 Mar 1905, New Castle, Henry County, Indiana, United States

Died: 26 Dec 1988, Indianapolis, Marion County, Indiana, United States

Father: George G. Ballard (01 Feb 1878 – 26 Dec 1956)

Mother: Catherine (Wilkison) Ballard (22 Aug 1869 – 15 Feb 1952)

Siblings: Martha (1909 – 1993), Marian M. (1912 – 1996), George M. (1917 – 1998)

Spouse: Carl G. Diekman

Married: 04 Dec 1920

Children: Carl Junior, Lou Anna

Profession: Store Clerk and Homemaker

Marie Diekman, circa 1920

LOU ANNA DIEKMAN

Born: 13 Mar 1927, New Castle, Henry County, Indiana, United States

Died:

Father: Carl G. Diekman

Mother: Margaret Marie Ballard

Siblings: Carl Junior

Spouse: Robert George Van Zant

Married: 13 May 1951

Children: Rex Alan, Katherine Ann, Robert Scott

Profession: Office Worker and Homemaker

Lou Anna Diekman, 1944

Sources

In addition to the writings and recollections of the author, the following source materials were used in the preparation of this work.

Written Sources

*Letters, photos, written records and documents, and newspaper clippings from the Van Zant and Diekman families

*Microfilm issues of the New Castle *Daily Courier* and *Daily Times* from October 14, 16, 17, 18, 19, 20, 23, 25, November 11, 1911; February 20, 22, 23, 24, 26, 1912

*Indiana State Prison Records, Indiana State Archives, Indianapolis, Indiana

*Radford, Darrel. *New Castle, Indiana: A Pictorial History*. St. Louis: G. Bradley Publishing; 1992

Oral Interviews

*The following individuals were interviewed by the author between 1992 and 1997: Carl George Diekman, Cressy George Hessler, Marie Anna (Diekman) Hiatt, Leroy Hiatt, Marian M. (Ballard) Rhodes, Lou Anna (Diekman) Van Zant, Robert George Van Zant

Internet Sources

*The following internet site was utilized: www.ancestry.com

About the Author

Scott Van Zant grew up as a sixth generation resident of Henry County, Indiana. He currently lives in Pittsburgh, Pennsylvania and teaches at The University of Findlay.

The author of several research articles in the health professions, *Histories From My Heartland* is his first book.